KU-495-693

Karina Has Down Syndrome
One Family's Account of the Early Years with a Child who has Special Needs

Cheryl Rogers and Gun Dolva

Jessica Kingsley Publishers
London and Philadelphia

All rights reserved. No paragraph of this publication may be reproduced, copied or transmitted save with written permission of the Copyright Act 1956 (as amended), or under the terms of any licence permitting limited copying issued by the Copyright Licensing Agency, 33–34 Alfred Place, London WC1E 7DP. Any person who does any unauthorised act in relation to this publication may be liable to prosecution and civil claims for damages.

The right of Cheryl Rogers to be identified as author of this work has been asserted by him in accordance with the Copyright, Designs and Patents Act 1988.

First published in 1998 by Southern Cross University Press

This edition published in the United Kingdom in 1999 by
Jessica Kingsley Publishers Ltd,
116 Pentonville Road, London
N1 9JB, England
and
325 Chestnut Street,
Philadelphia PA 19106, USA.

www.jkp.com

© Copyright Cheryl Rogers 1998 and 1999

20279906

Library of Congress Cataloging in Publication Data
A CIP catalog record for this book is available from the Library of Congress

British Library Cataloguing in Publication Data
Rogers, Cheryl
Karina has Down Syndrome : one family's account of the early years with a child who has special needs 1. Down syndrome – Popular works 2. Down syndrome – Patients – Australia – Biography
I. Title II. Dolva, Gun
362.1'9892858842'0092

ISBN 1 85302 820 7

Printed and Bound in Great Britain by
Athenaeum Press, Gateshead, Tyne and Wear

To Danika, Karina and Joshua

"These days we look more at Karina herself and less at what she can or cannot do. We try to do this with all our children."

Gun Dolva and Rodney Potter

"Down Syndrome is an irreversible condition present at birth due to a chromosomal abnormality. It is the single most common cause of intellectual disability. There are other associated features varying in degree and occurrence. These may include a characteristic appearance, low body tone and heart abnormality. It occurs in one in every 800 births in WA."

Down Syndrome Association of Western Australia Inc.
c1986

FOREWORD

Down Syndrome, the commonest cause of intellectual disability in our community, affects about 25 children born in Western Australia each year. This wonderful book tells us about the impact of that simple statistic on one family.

In describing the first six years of Karina's life, Gun and Rodney have provided us with a wealth of information about what they have found useful, at all times stressing that this is their experience, and it may not suit everyone. There is no sense of their way being the right way — it is simply one way, and a way they share selflessly with us. That individuals do not always see eye to eye is acknowledged, not as a difficulty, but merely as a difference. For me, it is this emphasis on each person's uniqueness that is the highlight of this book — it underpins the way Gun and Rodney approach all their children, their family and friends, the health profession, their life.

Some families who have a baby with a disability feel anger, questioning why this has happened to them; others are critical of medical and support services or lack of appropriate services, and some feel guilt or anxiety about coping with a child with a disability. While we understand each of these responses, it is often difficult for those outside the immediate family to know how to react, what to say, how best to help, what to do and, at times, things are said and done which are not at all helpful. Reading this book will give us all insight into some of these difficulties, and some of the solutions.

Almost everyone knows a person with Down Syndrome. I therefore commend this book as a source of inspiration to you all: close and extended family members, friends, health professionals, support agencies and people in the community who are likely to come in contact with people with Down Syndrome or their families. Not only will it provide you with valuable information, it is a well-told story that is a great pleasure to read.

Dr Carol Bower
Medical Officer at the WA Birth Defects Registry
King Edward Memorial Hospital
Head of the Division of Epidemiology
TVW Telethon Institute for Child Health Research

And then my heart with pleasure fills,
And dances with the daffodils.

W Wordsworth

CONTENTS

Introduction

There is something wrong with our baby.

I cannot believe what the paediatrician is saying. He is asking Rodney and I what we know about Down Syndrome.

He says there is a possibility Karina has been born with it. She has a number of characteristics — a small head that is flatter than usual at the back, swollen eyes with a mongoloid slant, floppy muscle tone.

I hear myself telling him he can't be certain. To me she simply has many of the solid features of both our families.

He says he is 95 per cent sure she has Down Syndrome.

•

The paediatrician speaks softly, leaning towards us in his chair as though ready to catch us if we fall.

It is winter, late morning, and Rodney and I are seated by a humidicrib in the neonatal ward at Princess Margaret Hospital for Children, in Perth.

Karina, born at home last night, is asleep in my arms. She has just finished breast-feeding.

Believing that her admission to hospital a few hours after birth had simply been a precaution, to help her over one of the small hurdles many new babies face, we have come to take her home.

Rodney will tell me later that by then he had begun to suspect there might be something more seriously wrong, but I am still "riding high" on the euphoria that most mothers experience after giving birth.

There had been nothing extraordinary about this pregnancy, not even the "sense that something is wrong" that many mothers who go on to deliver a healthy baby claim to feel.

I was healthy, 33, and we already had a "normal" three and a half year old daughter. Down Syndrome had seemed such a low risk it was not worth thinking about, so I am totally unprepared for a diagnosis that will change all our lives. It all seems so unreal.

The full impact of the paediatrician's words take a long time to sink in.

What sort of future can our baby expect? And us? Will we have a baby forever? How will we manage?

These are just some of the questions we find ourselves asking, part of the fear and confusion that overwhelms us in the weeks that follow.

•

That diagnosis was six years ago. Social workers, support agency staff, other parents and — most importantly — Karina herself, have taught us a lot since then about what it means to live with a disability like Down Syndrome.

Some days are not easy and some days are exhausting, but there are some wonderful times as well. Karina's spontaneous joy and her easygoing, enthusiastic, friendly nature is worth bottling. While her disability is a nuisance, Karina herself is a real treasure, and we consider ourselves lucky to have her.

Every minor milestone marks a major achievement which we never, ever take for granted. This applies to Karina, our elder daughter, Danika, and our son, Joshua, who was born three years after Karina.

Along the way we have learned a lot about the approach needed to help Karina achieve developmental goals. We have also gathered a lot of information which we hope may be useful to new parents in the situation we were in six years ago, carers involved with young Down Syndrome children and the wider community in which Karina now plays an active part.

From our own experience, and from talking to other parents and carers of children with disabilities, we know the need for support and information is highest in these challenging early years. Often it is the experience of other families that is of most practical use.

That is how this book came about. It is not intended as a definitive guide — parenting is such a personal challenge and every child is so different that each family must work out what works best for them. In the words of the philosopher, Friedrich Nietzsche: "This is my way; what is your way? *The* way doesn't exist".

Karina's story is our family's account of living day to day with a child who has some special needs.

1

Daffodils and Tears

Karina's planned home birth, two weeks before her due date, is reassuringly ordinary.

High on endorphins and with my glasses off, it is the daffodils I will remember most about this afternoon. A pot of blooms on the bedroom window sill catches the winter sunlight to become a wonderful haze of colour, setting me off quoting from Wordsworth's *I Wandered Lonely as a Cloud*, as Karina's arrival draws nearer.

It is 7.05pm on 2 August 1990 when our new daughter slips into the world amidst relief, joy and jubilation. After an 11 hour 20 minute labour, best described as sheer hard work, the only mild surprise is her sex.

I had half convinced myself that it was a boy this time — a brother for our three and a half year old daughter, Danika — but here we have another beautiful daughter.

I am surprised, and overjoyed. Unlike her dark haired sister, she has a cap of fine, blonde hair, reminiscent of my Swedish background. Her solid features are remarkably similar to those of Rodney's father.

Soon afterwards I have a shower and, while Rodney takes our new daughter out of the room to introduce her to her grandparents and sister, I help our midwife, Jill, make the bed.

I give Karina her first breastfeed. She feeds beautifully and as I lie in bed cuddling her, Rodney cracks open the champagne and we all celebrate her arrival.

It is one and a half hours before the first clear signs that our baby may not be well begin to show ... it is a further 16 hours before we learn Karina might have Down Syndrome.

When I go back over the details of the delivery, there is little to suggest that there might be something different about our baby. Towards the end of the second stage of labour, her heartbeat had suddenly dropped from its regular 120 beats per minute, prompting Jill to quickly urge me to push. Rodney had wiped yet another cool flannel across my forehead as I gave one last push, and Karina had made her entrance.

Jill says later that at that time there were no indications that she ought to be particularly concerned for the baby. The clinical signs had simply given her the message "get the baby out". Had the heartbeat been alright, she would have let me take my time with this last part of the birthing.

Immediately she is born I hold our latest small miracle close to inspect her. It passes through my mind how "floppy" she is ... I don't remember Danika being this way ... but I am curious rather than concerned. There are so many more positive signs to enjoy.

Although two weeks early, Karina is as plump and pink as any full term baby. The birth has been a beautiful experience and she appears strong and alert. When Jill clears our baby's throat, she lets out a cry and begins to breathe independently. Any suspicion that this is not the healthy child we expected to have does not surface.

Karina's Apgar score goes from a good 8 at birth to an excellent 10 at 10 minutes. She weighs in at 3150 grams, is 49cm long, her heart rate quickly settles at 115 beats per minute, and her basal body temperature is a normal 36 degrees. Her length and weight are almost exactly the same as Danika's (49cm and 3200g) at birth.

Ninety minutes after delivery, some of the first warning signs begin to appear. Karina's body temperature and heart rate start to drop. When I feed her at 9pm her temperature and heart rate are borderline, indicating to Jill how crucial it is to keep her warm and under observation. Jill rarely leaves a home for at least four hours after a birth, and though she remembers being vigilant, she is *always* vigilant in the first few hours.

Jill tells us later that she had hoped Karina would warm up after having a feed and being tucked in beside me in bed, but by 10.30pm, she is colder and her heart rate slower. Jill by this time is very concerned for Karina's life and knows we need medical expertise. She immediately telephones Princess Margaret Hospital to let them know she is bringing in the baby for what we think is a routine check.

She musters help from Rodney's mother. Shirley has travelled to Perth from Mandurah with his father, John, to be here for the birth and to help in the hectic days immediately afterwards. It is decided that Rodney and I will stay at home with Danika and John, so we can get some sleep. I am confident we will collect Karina from the hospital tomorrow morning, when this temporary hiccup will be behind her, so I sleep well that night.

That will come to sound bizarre later, but right now it seems a very natural thing to do.

•

We learn later that Karina was very actively dealt with by the admitting doctors. She strongly resisted attempts to introduce a tube to her throat and so that was quickly abandoned.

Jill found Karina's defiance reassuring:

> It showed there was plenty of life in this little girl. I was also very relieved that her grandmother was with her ... I remember feeling very comfortable trusting Karina to Shirley on the trip into hospital and letting Gun and Rodney rest.

Karina quickly responded to oxygen being administered and was then transferred to a humidicrib in the neonatal unit to bring her body temperature back to normal. Her singlet was cut off, her nappy removed and blood samples were taken. Two photographs were also taken, as happens in such cases where there is the chance the baby might not survive.

•

It is in the admitting area that one of the doctors first suggests that our daughter might have some kind of syndrome. Jill later says she believes that was the first time she considered the possibility herself. She and Shirley decide not to tell us, but rather to wait and let the paediatrician tell us himself in the morning.

I telephone the hospital early to check on Karina's condition. A nurse tells me she is doing alright, but is not a well little girl. Immediately I feel somehow guilty ... does the nurse consider me negligent for not being in hospital with my baby?

I am still blissfully ignorant. Remarkably, I am too overwhelmed by the positive experience of the birth itself and my lovely little girl to worry about this "routine" check-up. As far as I am concerned, Karina has merely had a minor setback after the birth and is in hospital as a precaution. Rodney and I have a happy and relaxed breakfast before leaving for the hospital. It is about 8.30am and I feel well, moving quite comfortably.

All our joy and jubilation of last night is a stark contrast to our feelings upon seeing Karina this morning.

Our baby arrived into the world in a happy and warm home environment. Now, here she is in a plastic humidicrib in a brightly lit neonatal unit, connected to tubes and wires. It seems so artificial and unnecessary ... I am still having trouble realising something is really wrong.

The hospital staff could not be more caring. They arrange a room for us and help us settle in; throughout the next few days they are always available to answer our questions. They handle all the babies in the neonatal ward with such love and care that we feel totally reassured that everything that can be done for Karina is being done. The other babies in the ward seem so tiny and frail, while she looks so pink, fat and well nourished that we're not unduly concerned for her safety.

I remove Karina from the humidicrib to breastfeed her while we wait for the paediatrician,. He seems to take forever to get to us and when he does, his news is numbing. He says there is the possibility she has a chromosomal disorder, such as Down Syndrome. It is only after he describes its visual symptoms, which Karina shares, that we begin to believe he might be right.

On the fringes of my vision I notice another midwife and other people around us. They seem to drift in and out of my consciousness, looking shocked, sad, and as though they want to do something to help us. Time seems suspended. I calmly hand Karina to a nurse, then Rodney and I go to the room staff have prepared for us and cry. We cry more than we have ever cried before, and more than we ever do again.

That afternoon the doors of the neonatal ward open and Jill walks in, carrying a huge bunch of golden daffodils. This will become one of my most cherished and enduring memories of this time – an incredibly refreshing sight. She has remembered me quoting Wordsworth yesterday, and has brought with her some of the sunshine that still exists beyond our cocoon of grief.

2

Keeping Us Afloat: Family and Friends

The chromosome test confirms the diagnosis: Karina has that extra bit of chromosome 21 that makes a Trisomy 21 child. The good news is that she is alive, alert and active, and her heart, hearing and sight seem fine.

The hours and days after that initial diagnosis are the worst in our lives. I cry more ... why had this happened to us? Shocked and confused, we mourn the death of the child we had assumed I had given birth to, yet dearly love the baby we have. We want our child, but don't want her to have Down Syndrome. We love Karina and are so determined to have her home, that the hospital staff allow us to take her as soon as she is strong enough.

By the time the results of the chromosome tests arrive, we have begun to accept the disability. In many ways, accepting that Karina had been born with Down Syndrome is made easier by having had the home birth. We remember her birth with joy, and nothing can ever replace the first precious hours we had with her, before the diagnosis. Before then everything seemed normal, and we believed we had a "normal" baby.

As well as dealing with our own feelings, we now have to tell our families.

Shirley of course had known that first night, though we did not realise this until after we arrived at the hospital the next morning. All night she had carried the knowledge of what we were yet to find out, and Rodney will later say that he had been puzzled as to why his mother seemed so upset

7

that morning. I had merely thought she was upset that Karina had to go into hospital for a while. When we arrive home she gives Rodney a letter in which she expresses her grief and feelings.

Telling the family is hard. Their distress at what they see as their own loss makes it all seem so much worse.

I find it difficult to know how to respond to well meant blunders like "perhaps it would have been better if she had just slipped away". The equally well intended handouts from religious groups, pointing out that we have been "chosen" to care for this special child, seem trite — almost sick — at a time when we are understandably sensitive.

And how do we tell our friends? To telephone and casually announce "The baby's a girl, and by the way she has Down Syndrome" is too flippant, yet to go into a slow and detailed explanation over and over again would only add to the agony we already feel.

Eventually, I write a long letter, addressed to all my friends. It breaks the news, explains the medical condition, and attempts to describe my feelings ...

... How can I tell you that my beautiful baby has Down Syndrome.

Karina has no strong physical features of Down Syndrome. Her nose bridge is perhaps a little flatter than most, but she is more beautiful than most other children. Since she does not have an enlarged tongue she has no problem with feeding or swallowing. Her muscle tone is a little more floppy than in most children but she is active and kicks and screams like any other child.

These children are also prone to heart troubles, but Karina has an excellent heart. Common illnesses are supposed to affect Down's children more than other children, but with good general health there is no reason she should suffer from this.

They do however need more help to achieve goals. As they grow they now frequently enter normal school where teachers' aides help them develop to their potential.

And when they leave school the emphasis is on independent living and a career that fits their abilities. Just like any other child.

... The hardest thing for me to overcome is all the accumulated preconceptions about handicapped children. And this is where a lot of us are caught up. But living with Karina now, and looking to the future, I hold the same aspirations for her as for Danika. I want them both to find happiness and success in their lives ...

In the end, I get as far as sealing the envelopes, but the letters are never posted. It doesn't matter — the writing helps me sort out my own feelings as part of coming to terms with what had happened, and will remain a therapeutic activity for me.

When I do eventually get around to telephoning my friends, their generally calm reaction is a welcome relief from the intense feelings we are caught up in. Perhaps they can afford to be calm — after all, it was not a member of their family who has been born with Down Syndrome. But at a time when all around us seems surreal, their support and normality help keep us afloat.

3

Help

Karina remains in hospital only three days. We are keen to have her home.

It is in the discharge room attached to the neonatal ward that we have our first contact with a social worker — our first link with the many support services for families like ours.

The social worker encourages us to contact the Down Syndrome Association, an organisation that will provide us with invaluable early support. Most of its members have a child who has Down Syndrome, so they know better than most what new families might be going through.

It is a relief, in these early weeks, to be visited by a couple from the Association with their two children, one of whom has Down Syndrome. It is reassuring to see that having such a child is not a big problem for them.

The weeks after Karina's birth are like a whirlwind, with constant appointments. For the first two or three months we see some sort of specialist, social trainer or support service once or twice a week — and all while we are still in shock. Any thought of me returning to outside work, at least for now, is out of the question.

All this activity is good though; it means we keep talking and have emotional support while we are still learning what it means to have a baby with Down Syndrome.

Despite this, I find it very hard, at first, to take Karina out. Having Danika means it is not long after the birth that

I reluctantly rejoin the daily rush of mothers ferrying children to school. Anxieties about being the mother of a baby with a disability surface ... how do I tell people she has Down Syndrome?

The first day I return to the school run I find myself leaving Karina in her car capsule; I am uncertain about how other people might react to her — and unsure how I might respond to their reactions. It does not take much these days to reduce me to tears.

Inevitably, word spreads that our new baby is in the car, and a small crowd gathers to inspect her. It is a tremendous relief to see how unconcerned yet curious other people are about her Down Syndrome; the reaction I dread is in my mind, no-one else's. As we continue to take Karina out with us, we find that — if anything — more total strangers approach us to admire her than would have done if she did not have a disability. I cannot go shopping without someone stopping to chat, and this will continue for a further three years. It opens my eyes to the reality of just how many people have contact with those with a disability.

One of the most touching gestures happens when Karina is just a few weeks old. We are at a Buddhist restaurant to celebrate a friend's birthday, and the restaurant owners recognise that she has Down Syndrome. They spend a little time with us, then return after we have finished our meal with a gift: a piece of red prayer thread that has been blessed by the Dalai Lama. It touches us very much that they have chosen to give Karina something that is obviously so precious to them.

When she is six weeks old I enrol her in a local day-care centre. She goes on to spend several hours a week there after I return to part-time work and study, and although I find it terribly hard to take her along that first day, it turns out to be one of the best decisions I could make. She benefits from the caring support she receives there, particularly from one staff member who has a special interest in working with babies with disabilities.

Just as important for me at this time, is the way in which Karina is so readily accepted. I am almost apologetic, fearing we might be turned away, that a Down Syndrome baby might be seen as too much to cope with, but Karina could not be made more welcome. This reaffirms my hope that she will also be accepted in the general community.

As well as helping her, the day-care staff provide me with invaluable support. I no longer feel so isolated caring for Karina, and day-care becomes a vital extension to our support network.

I will come to see that I needed to believe she had a future in the community, that life would hold some hope for her. Once I believe that, I can start to help her achieve her potential.

I also see later that in those early weeks I was probably so immersed in learning all I could about Down Syndrome, that I was getting a biased view of the world. I start to recognise this because after three or four months I feel ready to relax my grip on the Association a little, and go back to the world as I once knew it.

Although I eventually accept that we will never "get over it", we do get better and better at living with Down Syndrome, and I come to regret now that I failed to make better use of other wonderful support services and agencies in the early years. Work and family take up so much of my time though ... I quite simply overlook the fact that we all might benefit from some outside help. It seems easier to push on than to go to the trouble of organising another new thing.

I also fall into the trap of feeling there are plenty of families far more deserving than ours. Having a child with a disability has made us more aware of the range of disabilities in the community, and how tough some can be on the families involved. Compared to some people, our situation does not seem all that bad, or so we tell ourselves — later I will realise that this "stiff upper lip" attitude is a liability. It stifles our call for much needed help, and we push ourselves to the edge of our limits of physical, mental and emotional strength.

It will be three more years, when I am back working part-time, studying part-time, and have Danika at school and newborn Joshua, before I even consider we can use some help. By this time Karina will have become an extremely active toddler, and I will be exhausted. At the suggestion of a Disabilities Services social trainer, who not only suggests the need for help but kindly follows it through and organises it for me, I finally begin using the services available.

Once Rodney and I overcome our hesitancy about using this assistance, we will have Home Help, a subsidised service organised by our local Community Support Group, for two hours a fortnight. When I am ill and unable to care for Karina and Joshua on my own, and no other family member or friend is available to help, we will call upon Crisis Care to look after the children until Rodney can get home.

We will use a psychologist, available through Disability Services, when we need support to help us through critical stages (such as after Joshua is born, when I am learning to balance the erratic behaviour of an active toddler with a new baby) and day-care centres. Once Karina starts school, before- and after-school care becomes an important part of our support network.

We will also use a home care and sitter service, available to us through Activ Foundation, when we need the occasional night off or weekend away. Once or twice a year, Rodney and I will stay at the appropriately named Carers' Retreat, a unit by the river in South Perth, and as Karina grows older, respite services will be more accessible to us.

Other people tell me now how "marvellous" they thought I was to have coped throughout those years, and although I accept their compliments, I actually consider myself just plain stupid not to have made better use of the available help long before I did. Sometimes the hardest thing to do is to make a phone call and say "I have a disabled child and I am having a really hard time. Can you help?"

A cranky, tired heroine is no good to anybody, but it is some quirky facet of human nature that applauds us for being martyrs. It is perplexing that people ask "How are you doing?" and expect only a positive reply — yet an honest reply risks the socially unacceptable tag of "whinger".

Services are there to be used by the families they were designed for, otherwise the funding dries up and the service dies, benefiting no-one. Although I will learn not to feel I am a lesser person when I ask for help, in these early days it is not something I know how to do.

4

Reminders on the Fridge

After the first three months a pattern gradually emerges and we become more used to the frequent medical appointments. We enrol Karina with The Authority for Intellectually Handicapped Persons – more commonly known as Irrabeena, and later as the Disability Services Commission. (To save confusion, from here on I shall refer to this wonderful support agency as Disability Services.)

Disability Services is State government funded and runs an Early Intervention Program aimed at servicing the needs of babies and young children with disabilities, and helping them develop to their potential.

We find the program invaluable, both for what it helps Karina achieve and what it shows us we can contribute to her development and enjoyment of life.

We will learn that most children teach their parents how to play the games that are important to child development. A little face peering around the corner of a cupboard, for example, prompts a parental "boo!", and immediately one of the cause-and-effect games necessary for language development has begun. Most children lure their parents into doing this without anyone being conscious of the theory.

Before our experiences with Karina make us more conscious of the theory behind child's play, we do not really explore its significance. We don't need to – Danika's development had progressed so rapidly and naturally that we seldom gave it a second thought. We realise quite quickly however that Karina will not be initiating the games necessary for her development at anything like the same rate. It is thanks partly to Disability Services staff and the Early Intervention Program that we learn many of the skills needed to lead and prompt her.

Our first contact with Disability Services is in August 1990, when she is 18 days old. Staff there organise for her to be assessed by an occupational therapist, a speech therapist, and a physiotherapist. It seems like a lot of "ists" but we accept their advice that Karina be visited at home, initially by a physiotherapist once a week. The physio will work on a program of developmentally appropriate exercises to maximise Karina's rate of general development, and the reasons for each exercise will be explained so we can continue them at home between each visit.

The routine that develops is reassuring after days of having to fit our lives around random appointments. Being involved in the program gives us hope — we feel now that we are moving on, starting to do the best we can for Karina.

(Six years later, a social trainer, representing all three therapies, remains our main contact, putting us in touch with specialists in the core areas as they are needed. Karina's development is regularly reassessed and new activities added as her skills improve.)

It soon becomes obvious that the real value of the physiotherapy and occupational therapy sessions is in what they show us we can do to help our daughter between each session. The real work begins after the trainer leaves, therefore I constantly seek ways to incorporate into our lives the activities that will make learning an enjoyable experience for Karina, and a natural part of the daily routine for the rest of the family.

It is important for me to be at each session, to listen, observe and ask questions. I also ask the trainer to write down in simple language the activities we can do before the next appointment. These suggestions go up on the refrigerator door, reminders in sharp black and white for later in the week when the memory will, inevitably, blur.

I feel this interaction is very important, and the physiotherapists and social trainers are not simply providing a service for us to tap into once each week — they are arming us with the skills we need to help Karina develop the strength, coordination and will to eventually be able to do things herself.

During this first year I keep a diary to record her main achievements and to jot down key words ("encourage rolling, lifting head" etc) to jog my memory about the areas considered most important by the trainers. This helps at a time when, like any new mother, I am extremely tired.

The notes on the refrigerator are also useful for Rodney. It is harder for him to incorporate the trainers' suggestions into our daily routine — he is, after all, the partner out earning a living for now, and therefore has less contact with Karina and the Disability Services staff than I do.

Sometimes I resent the extra work that has been thrust upon me simply because I am the "primary carer". I see my life becoming more and more involved with Karina's special needs — a far different role than my involvement with the "normal" needs of Danika. Sometimes it all seems too daunting. This is not what I originally planned to do with my life.

Rodney and I talk about this a lot, helping us both to come to terms with the slightly altered direction our lives have taken. There is no substitute for good communication in a marriage and having a child with a disability emphasises this. In our case, it will make our relationship stronger, to the benefit of all our children.

5

Babies Are Not Born Walking

Parents of children who do not have a developmental delay observe and rejoice as each obvious milestone is reached. Crawling. The first step. The first word. Success on the potty! Our pride as each seemingly small step towards independence is achieved can take us by surprise.

For parents of a child like Karina, it is different.

We spend much of our time encouraging the multitude of minor goals that must be achieved on the way to each big step, and learn never to take the little things for granted. They are the foundation for further achievements.

When Karina first holds up her head, and briefly looks around her, it is to our thrill and cries of delight. It means she is one step closer to exploring her world, and we eagerly telephone our families and friends to share the news.

Sometimes it is hard, but eventually we try less and less to compare her slow development with that of other children. Comparisons are good when they are just that, but they can cause frustration and sadness when a child has a developmental delay.

We will learn to look more at Karina herself and what she does, and less at what she perhaps should achieve or cannot do. Each minor step towards each milestone is rejoiced, as is each hug and smile. We do this with all our children. While we always keep the milestones in mind, we set no fixed time limit on their achievement.

Karina will reach most of the milestones other children reach, but not necessarily at the same time or in the same order. This is partly because her learning cues are blurred and she is not able to understand or remember things as well as most children do. She is long-sighted, has coloboma (an incomplete retina) in her right eye, and reduced hearing, though just how much is hard to test accurately. All these things considered, it is understandable that she takes much longer to learn.

We accept her problems and work with her at her rate.

Karina's early development can be plotted through my diary, Disability Services reports, and notes made at each visit by staff from the service.

21 November 1990:

Karina is now three and a half months old. She is "gooing" a lot and last month smiled for the first time. I cannot help comparing her slow rate of development with Danika's at the same age.

She can now hold her head unsupported for a moment when resting against my shoulder, so we are encouraging her to do this more.

To strengthen her neck muscles and so encourage better head control, I clasp her hands and gently bring her forward and up from lying on her back. It's a game we also do at nappy change time.

She is still very "floppy" and does not move her head to the middle or from side to side at all when she is lying on her back. I have started using bright, noisy, attractive toys to encourage her to focus on objects on either side of her head and follow their slow movement up and down and from side to side. By turning both her eyes and her face towards an object moving this way she will become more aware of her body in space, which is necessary if she is eventually to learn to roll over.

She attempts to roll to the left and right only when lying on her side. We are spending quite a lot of time teaching and encouraging her to roll; by supporting her and holding her legs and hips and moving her arms and head, we take her from her back to her side then over on to her tummy, over and over again.

We are also encouraging her to clasp her hands together, when lying on her back and side, to develop her awareness of her mid-line.

I notice that Karina hates being "stuck" on her tummy where she cannot see around her. At least when she is on her back she can see something of her surroundings. I have to fight my instinct to prop her up on pillows to relieve her frustration at not being able to move, for if I do all the work for her all the time, it will take a lot longer for her to develop the strength, coordination and will to move around by herself.

I carry Karina around in a "monkey grip", her body resting along the length of my arm with her face looking outwards and her arms and legs hanging down. She is well supported this way, and it is more stimulating for her than the standard carrying position where her face would be buried into my shoulder.

Karina's eyesight appears poor. She does not look directly at objects. I must remember to have her eyes checked soon.

21

14 December 1990:

Mum looked after the girls so Rodney and I could go shopping, and made a breakthrough with Karina's feeding. She found it quicker and easier to give Karina her formula from a spoon than from the bottle, "dribbling" the formula into her mouth then stroking her throat to encourage her to swallow, just as you would stroke a kitten to swallow a pill.

When Karina is not with me to breastfeed, she is bottle-fed. Bottle-feeding her is always slow at first because her poor muscle control and coordination means it is hard for her to wrap her tongue easily around the teat. For babies with an enlarged tongue — one of the characteristics of Down Syndrome which Karina fortunately does not have — this must be even harder.

I am trying a new type of teat each week. Nothing seems to work — they are all too hard for her to suck. For a few weeks at least we have some success using the thumb of a rubber glove pulled over the top of the feed bottle. It is soft enough for Karina, and the formula simply dribbles through a hole in the thumb and into her mouth.

After Mum's discovery, other people begin using the spoon method when feeding Karina. They find it a lot easier than the bottle.

These feeding problems are one reason I breastfeed Karina until she is 18 months old. After she has latched on, the milk "lets down" and into her mouth. As her muscle control increases, feeding becomes less of a problem.

17 December 1990:

Karina is now four and a half months old and "has music wherever she goes" thanks to the bells tied to her wrists and ankles. We also put socks on her feet with faces or bells attached to them. She appears to be moving her arms and legs deliberately to make the bells tinkle. This is all helping to make her aware of her body in space.

Now when Karina rolls from her back on to her tummy, we lift her trunk up slightly to allow her to pull out her arm.

18 December 1990:

Went Christmas shopping. Came home, unloaded car, put shopping away – and 10 minutes later realised Karina was still in the garage in her capsule! She is so quiet and undemanding sometimes, and does not move about much, so it is all too easy to forget she is there.

8 January 1991:

Everyone in tears at nappy time. This hot weather is not helping Karina's constipation, which is agony for her and heart-wrenching for us. She screams through each bowel motion, which happens only every two to three days.

We give her more water but drinking from a teat is slow and difficult for her.

Baby massage and "bicycling" exercises that work so well for most babies don't seem to help Karina at all. All we can do is nurse her through it.

> *As a last resort we sometimes put a few drops of infant laxative into a bottle. We only use this when things get really bad, as do not want to make her dependent upon it.*

Like many babies with Down Syndrome, Karina does not wake up demanding to be fed even though she is hungry. We have to wake her to make sure she gets the fluid and food she so badly needs.

At around six months, well before she can anticipate the "punch line" of games, she anticipates the pain of a bowel motion and starts screaming five to 10 minutes before.

As a toddler she has to constantly have plenty of water to sip. We try adding more fibre to her diet, using herbal teas, prune juice and other remedies. Few seem to help.

This continues, particularly in hot weather, until Karina has stronger bowel muscles. It also gets easier once she is better able to drink, and so drinks more.

As she grows older, there is an improvement when she drinks unassisted and willingly, and can tell us when she is thirsty.

> *14 January 1990:*
>
> *We are spending a lot of time encouraging her to lift her head, and to roll from side to side.*
>
> *I lie on my tummy facing Karina, who is lying on her tummy, and call to her to try to get her to look up at me. A rolled up nappy, under her chest, gives her some support.*

I also encourage her to lift her head from the downwards facing position when she is lying over my arm.

Another "giggling game" is to sit her astride my leg, tipping her from side to side to encourage her to hold up her head.

12 February 1991:

Karina has begun taking more notice of other children at day-care.

13 February 1991:

Karina is now just over seven months old and I am very concerned about her slow rate of progress.

The development of her head control seems particularly slow. When we move a noisy toy slowly across in front of her it is almost as though she is blinkered, noticing it when it is directly in front of her but unable to coordinate her head and eye movement to track it.

This is why we are now trying to encourage Karina to look between two objects, shaking one then the other to see if she will look towards it. We are starting with noisy toys, then will try toys that are not noisy. We will also continue encouraging her to follow slow moving objects with her eyes – up, down, across and around. Looking at toys that drop to the ground and hitting toys on surfaces are other suggested games we are now trying, along with "peek a boo" with a sheet of paper.

Karina seems to have made no gains when lying on her tummy.

One method we are still using to try to encourage her to move her head involves me lying on my back on the floor with Karina on my tummy, facing me while I am talking to her.

We also prop her chest up on a rolled up towel with toys in front of her. This lifts her chest and shoulders off the floor and aims to make it easier and therefore more interesting for her to practise using her arms and hands to lift herself.

She is happy on her back, gooing and grabbing at her feet now and pushing her feet off any available surface. From a side lying position she is just starting to push herself into the last stage of a roll on to her back.

Her head no longer lags much when we pull her up into the sitting position.

19 February 1991:

It is reassuring to see the younger babies at day-care. They too seem helpless. Babies are not born walking! Perhaps Karina is not so far behind after all.

3 March 1991:

Lying in bed, Karina looked up at me and smiled.

6 *March 1991:*

Karina rolled from her back to her front many times today, and did a front to back "flop". She can also now follow an object with her eyes and her head when held in a sitting position.

10 *March 1991:*

Karina followed a dropped object with her eyes and head. She also examined her sleeping sister thoroughly, with touching and soft noises.

12 *March 1991:*

Karina is up on her elbows, looking around. She reaches out to touch objects, even when they are not shaken to catch her attention.

15 *March 1991:*

Progress! Karina has started to roll from her back to her front, and occasionally from her front to her back.

She has also begun propping up on her forearms and lifting her head when lying on her tummy, supported by the rolled towel. Occasionally she will push herself up on one extended arm.

We are continuing to encourage her to look up at objects or faces when on her tummy or the towel. I get down on my knees, talking to her, to try to get her to look up at my face and follow it from side to side.

27

We are also trying to get her to take some of her weight through her (straight) arms when she is supported on the rolled towel wedge, and through her elbows when on the floor.

To help her get better at rolling from her front to her back we attract her attention, then get her to follow a toy in a semi-circle over her head so that she rolls. We tickle her arm if she seems to be finding it hard to move it across when she rolls.

We are also encouraging her to take some of her weight through her arms in front of her, and to look up at objects and faces when she is in a sitting position.

To encourage her to learn to get from her back to a sitting position, we roll her from her back to her right side, then hold her right thigh firm, pulling her gently up with her left arm so she props up on her extended right arm. Then we take hold of her hands and gently bring her forward into a supported sitting position.

We do this every time we pick her up. She has to help, so it is good exercise for her.

I discovered later that this is an excellent way in which to pick up a small child.

16 March 1991:

The car capsule is now too small for Karina, but she is not strong enough to sit unsupported in a child's car seat. We attempt to compensate by supporting her head on either side with towel "wedges".

Because she cannot sit up in a supermarket trolley, I take a pram mattress with us and lay her on it, with her head supported, in the front of the trolley.

(Today's child safety restraints are better designed to suit children with poor muscle tone and head control. These were not so readily available when Karina was a baby.)

4 April 1991:

We are trying reflexology. It is pleasurable for both Karina and for me, and seems to leave her more alert for a couple of days or so after each session. She shows most resistance and upset when her left foot is being worked on.

5 April 1991:

Karina can transfer toys from hand to hand, both ways. Everything goes to her mouth!

7 April 1991:

Karina is keen to interact with people. She watches faces and likes to touch them. She particularly enjoys being around other children.

16 April 1991:

She can support herself on one arm when lying on her tummy, but falls to her left. She is very interested in hands, sounds and faces. She loves cuddles.

19 April 1991:

Karina is eight and a half months old and can briefly raise her head and look around quite well now, when on her tummy. We are thrilled! We have phoned everyone to tell them. Staff at day-care are overjoyed.

She is also reaching for toys with her right hand and attempting to creep. Occasionally she rolls, unintentionally, on to her back from her tummy when she reaches for a toy and "flips" over.

Propped forward on her hands, or with her hands resting on her knees, she can sit for short periods before "flopping". We only try this on the carpet.

A 50cm orange ball has become our favourite exercise toy. We lie Karina over it on her tummy, roll it forwards or backwards until she touches the floor with her hands or her feet, then encourage her to take her weight accordingly. This also encourages her to look up.

We also move the ball from side to side, to encourage Karina to keep her head up and in the middle.

On her back, the same games encourage Karina to tuck in her chin.

We are not holding her weight (the ball is) so she can feel the effect of what she does. She loves it.

7 May 1991:

Karina is very interested in her own image in the mirror at day-care. She is sitting up better all the time.

13 May 1991:

She spends a lot of time looking, often kicking out when startled.

21 May 1991:

Karina is more alert. She can bang her hands down, track a falling object with her head and eyes and is much stronger in her back. She can now pull herself through 180 degrees while lying on her tummy. She is starting to play, copy, and seems more eager to "live". We think she is beginning to search for the toys we hide in peek-a-boo games.

24 May 1991:

We are now trying a peanut pillow to support her head in the car seat. Much better than the towel.

Now nine and a half months old, Karina is doing everything better. When we put her into the four-point kneeling position, she can hold herself momentarily before flopping.

We are now encouraging her to try to grasp small objects with her whole hand at first, then between her thumb and the side of her forefinger. Then we try to get her to release them.

Peek-a-boo with cloth and paper, finding half-hidden toys and banging hands or objects on to a surface are our other main "awareness" games. We are also using "poking" and "pointing" toys with dials and holes, and playdough.

The big ball is still one of our main exercise toys. We are also now encouraging Karina to reach out and up with one hand when sitting propped forward on her arms. To test her balance we move her a little in all directions when she sits with her hands on her knees.

27 May 1991:

Karina will now turn her head and body through 180 degrees to look at people when they talk. She is happier now when resting on her tummy than she was before.

28 May 1991:

Karina gums her way through part of a fruit bar. She manages to get it into her mouth most of the time, though her face is also covered in it.

30 May 1991:

The first tooth is through – front incisor, bottom right.

3 June 1991:

Karina can smack her lips together, put her fingers in her mouth, make "ba ba", "ma ma" sounds and loves banging toys on the table.

21 June 1991:

Now 10 and a half months old, Karina's hearing seems poor. I would like to have her hearing tested, but can it be done reliably when she does not always turn towards interesting sounds?

Karina still cannot hold her head up very long, although she tries, and still requires help to roll from her tummy to her back. She has rolled from front to back unaided three times in the past three weeks.

However, she does try to reach for toys when lying on her tummy, handles toys more, and kicks a lot, especially with her right leg. She also sits better and has started helping to push up and organise her legs when I help her from her back to the sitting position.

We are still encouraging her to reach out for toys when she is propped on her elbows, lying on her tummy, so that she learns how to roll over on to her back.

From the sitting position we are also still encouraging her to do this, so she learns to shift her weight and to rotate.

To get her to take her weight on her straight arms, I support her on her hands and knees over my calf, then lift her legs in the air.

An upturned crate with a toy on top keeps Karina occupied and provides some support so she can learn to stand for longer with her bottom tucked in and feet flat on the floor.

Comparisons with other children do not upset me so much now. The differences are so obvious. I have come to accept that Karina's development will be *slow, and am learning to look more at what she can do than what she can't.*

19 July 1991:

Everyone is very pleased with her progress. Although there have been no great gains, her movement has improved in the past month and she is much more alert and responsive.

Karina often obviously wants to sit up and is good at sitting, though she still sometimes falls over. She helps to initiate the "pull to sit" movement but lacks the strength to help much more.

She still dislikes four-point kneeling, however, and tends to push out of it with her legs. She also dislikes being on her tummy, and is not interested in standing.

We are trying Feldenkrais exercises and reflexology in a bid to enhance her development. Karina seems more alert after them and they help me too. I feel more relaxed and positive after each session.

We have introduced side-sitting into the exercise program, encouraging Karina to prop up on one arm (resting on her bottom), and play using the other. The next stage will be getting Karina on to her knees, ready for crawling, then standing up.

Side-sitting is the preferred position to sitting on her bottom at this stage, as allowing the latter could see her develop into a "bottom shuffler", further delaying her progress towards crawling, standing and eventually walking independently.

2 August 1991:

Karina's first birthday! Cause for celebration. Family, friends and godparents Malcolm and Sandra, together with Andrea and Paul joined us to mark this special milestone. Karina had cream and mashed birthday cake.

5 August 1991:

At day-care, Karina celebrated her birthday with the other children when staff strapped her comfortably into a chair so she could sit around the table with them. She is also doing jumping exercises there to help develop her leg muscles.

15 August 1991:

She really enjoys sitting, but still needs help to get there. She can turn around now to reach toys, when sitting, without falling over. She can also stand, with support.

We are continuing the sitting, side-sitting, four-point kneeling and standing exercises.

Karina is still waking up two or three times a night. Is she hungry, or is it habit?

Cost, time and distance have meant the end of Feldenkrais exercises and reflexology. I have come to realise I cannot do everything, yet still I feel guilty about it.

2 September 1991:

Karina is now starting to turn towards me when I call her name. This gives me such a buzz.

I now realise just how important her ability to mimic sounds and actions is to her development of language.

She has developed some prerequisite language skills – for example, she seems to enjoy playing with sounds and can make a variety of noises and consonant/vowel combinations such as "ma ma" and "ba ba". We have started introducing other sounds in repetitive games, as part of her preparation.

She will also occasionally join in action games such as clap hands and participate in turn-taking, although I am still not sure that she imitates. She is just starting to be aware that an object has gone when we remove it, but has not yet started searching for it.

Disability Services rates her skills at Level 2a and 2b on its Developmental Assessment record. This rating method is a tremendous confidence booster for me. It tells me that Karina is on her way to achieving some of the developmental milestones we expect children to reach, even though she is taking longer to get there. This in turn gives me the confidence to trust Disability Services trainers and to try their suggested activities, because they know where Karina is "at" developmentally and the activities that will benefit her most.

12 September 1991:

Thirteen months. We are home again after 10 days at Princess Margaret Hospital for Children. Karina had bronchiolitis. She is now going ahead in leaps and bounds and seems much more alert. It is taking me a little longer to adjust. After 10 days with her in hospital it seems strange to be back in the "real" world. Even going into the delicatessen to buy milk seems strange, almost threatening.

Karina can now push up on straight arms when on her tummy, but prefers to collapse to her elbows before reaching for a toy.

She really enjoys standing, and will stand up against the big play ball for five seconds or so before her legs collapse.

When sitting, she still does not like any movement that may cause her to topple over. She seems to be becoming aware of her centre of gravity, but is not yet able to adjust it.

23 September 1991:

Karina really enjoys the visits from Disability Services. She loves the attention.

She also enjoys shaking rattles, so we know she can hear, but we do not know how well. Her hearing is so hard to test. We do not know what she can or cannot hear, and she cannot tell us.

We spend a lot of time now on repetitive games. Little Peter Rabbit Has A Fly Upon His Nose (with actions) is a favourite. Karina needs the

*stimulation and appears to enjoy the sound, actions,
and the expectation of a possible tickle.*

14 October 1991:

We have now moved from the rented flat in
Joondanna to our own home in the hills, at
Darlington, on the block of land we bought when
expecting Danika. We are happy to be in our own
home in a quiet suburb. It is a good place for the
children and puts us closer to my mother, who helps
out. We swap to a new team of support service
providers.

30 October 1991:

I have stopped keeping reminder notes from the
sessions with the social trainers to prompt me through
each week because I find it easier to remember. The
terminology that once seemed so unfamiliar now
comes quite easily to me.

1 November 1991:

We have started using "controlled crying" in a bid
to get Karina to sleep through the night. She has
been waking several times each night but I am sure it
is habit. She only wants to nuzzle, not to feed. We
are exhausted.

7 November 1991:

We have waited until my part-time job is in recess
to try controlled crying properly. The first night I did

it all myself and was up virtually all night. Next morning I was ready to give up. It would have been impossible had I still been working. Rodney has agreed to take over some of the "night shift", but we are both aware that he must still get through the next day at work. Last night we put Karina to bed at 7.30pm. By 9pm she was awake again. Instead of picking her up, I went in and sat beside her cot, patting and talking quietly to her until she stopped crying. This took about 10 minutes. She was still awake when I left, and started crying within five minutes. I went back in and repeated the patting and talking for a further 10 minutes. It was very hard not to pick her up.

This went on until about 11pm when Karina at last fell asleep after a feed, probably through sheer exhaustion. She was not very hungry, reaffirming my suspicion that she is waking more from habit than from hunger. Rodney then took over. She woke again at 2am and all though the night, off and on, until morning. I gave her another feed at 6am.

We are even more exhausted, but know perseverance is the key to success.

8 November 1991:

Karina is now 15 months old and will clap hands in imitation. Rolling, to the left and right, is her only form of mobility.

Playing on her tummy, she can prop up on her forearms, push up on her fully extended arms and stretch her arms out fully in front of her to reach for toys. She is not yet moving forward on her tummy, though she tends to push backwards a little.

We are continuing with exercises designed to encourage her to creep and to crawl, placing her on her hands and knees as often as possible.

On her back she will rub her feet together, play with her feet and occasionally take her feet to her mouth.

She plays in the sitting position for quite long times now, with good stability, and she helps strongly when being transferred from the floor to a sitting position. Around her first birthday, we introduced her to the pleasures of play in the sitting position by propping her up with pillows to support her back and sides. This left her arms and legs free, without tiring her unduly, so that she could learn to reach out and get stronger.

She can bend her trunk forward well, and stretch out her arms to pick up toys on the floor in front of her, and rotate her trunk well to the left and right.

Although her equilibrium reactions appear to be developing she was apprehensive during a "row, row, row, the boat" game, when her centre of gravity was displaced backwards.

Karina will now transfer part-way from the sitting position towards the four-point kneeling position and can maintain that position momentarily when placed in it.

15 November 1991:

We have been very gradually introducing her to the taste of solids. At first we put a little mashed or pureed potato on to her tongue with a finger, then pushed her tongue into her mouth and closed it. We have started doing this regularly anyway, to get her out of the habit of sitting with her mouth open and her tongue out.

When spoon feeding Karina we put a little mashed food towards the back of her tongue, to encourage her to swallow. It is hard for her to move food from the front to the back of her mouth. I also stroke her throat, to help her swallow. Feeding her usually takes ages.

25 November 1991:

Karina is 15 months and three weeks old and has yet another cold. She is on antibiotics and anti-histamines. I am sure the constant colds have reduced her hearing.

Glasses have been prescribed for long-sightedness, but it is impossible to get her to keep them on. They are brought out only occasionally for interest. I wish I had more time to persevere.

She clearly understands the words "food", "Danika" and "Dad" when they are present. She will also now search out a toy or other object when it is removed from her sight. This shows that she understands that things exist even if she cannot see them.

She has also begun to try to imitate some gross motor movements, such as waving, and some movements involving finer hand coordination, such as opening a small box.

Today she keenly watched what the social trainer said and did, and occasionally tried to imitate her.

41

She also showed that she had some idea of cause-and-effect, using a music-maker toy with a string attached. She tried to get the social trainer to help her pull the string, trying to put the string in the trainer's hand.

Karina was described today as "a delightfully sociable little girl", although she tends to wait for others to initiate social contact rather than do so herself. She enjoys exploring new toys as well as social interaction games such as "peek-a-boo" and "round and round the garden" and has begun to laugh in anticipation of a tickle.

Although in general she does not consistently respond when her name is called, she is far more responsive when called by a familiar voice.

She also knows what a cup and spoon are used for, and understands "up you come" and "give baby a kiss" when accompanied by the appropriate gesture.

Gestures, vocalisations and crying are her means of communication. She is using sounds – "m", "d", "w", "u" and "a" – combined in babble (such as "mumu") and can produce a guttural sound.

She is now consolidating language skills at the nine to 12 month level

23 December 1991:

Controlled crying works! It took a while, but we got there. A full night's sleep is bliss. It took us two fortnightly sessions, interrupted by a 10 day break. The break allowed us to recover enough for the second attempt.

1 February 1992:

Karina is now enrolled for three full days on her own and one morning with me at Treetops Montessori Playgroup, Darlington. She loves it and they enjoy having her. When we first tried this playgroup late last year I felt she would benefit from the learning environment. It is very child-oriented, and reinforces a lot of the work we are doing to help her develop.

Breastfeeding has now been weaned down to 15 to 20 minutes per day. She has a bottle for fluids, and enjoys a wide variety of finger foods.

We have also begun placing Karina on the potty periodically and have had some success, mainly with bowel actions. It seems early to be starting potty training but, as with most things, we need to start Karina earlier than we would if she did not have a developmental delay.

6

Listen To Me

It may seem from the following that the exercises designed to help Karina's gross motor and fine motor development had by now been phased out in order to concentrate solely on her communications skills. Nothing could be further from the truth.

Motor development work dominated the first two years, because it was important to get Karina up and moving to explore her world. Although that emphasis gradually began to shift, we still spent a lot of time teaching her to haul herself up into the standing position on furniture, to crawl effectively, to avoid "bottom shuffling" and to "walk" with her feet on ours. We also played endless "fine motor" games such as mailing shapes, unscrewing lids and picking up sultanas.

While these exercises would continue, they simply became such an accepted part of everyday life that they no longer seemed remarkable enough to record.

14 February 1992:

Karina is 18 months old. She spends most of her time sitting and can reach for and play with toys such as her rattle. She can crawl short distances and I am hoping she will be walking by her second birthday.

Now that she is beginning to socialise, she is ready for her next stage in development – communication.

It is taking over from gross motor and fine motor development as our big project and is the logical next step on her path towards speech. Disability Services staff are putting a lot of effort into developing a speech program for Karina.

Children with Down Syndrome tend to be easygoing – happy to "go with the flow". Therefore it is often all too easy for others to speak for them, so they never learn to be responsible for the communication of their own needs and wants. This denies them the chance to develop speech, which in turn robs them of the chance to be more sociable and more generally accepted in the wider community. Allowing a child with a disability to "get away with" his or her own language, such as grunting, is not necessarily best for them.

Karina is now just entering the right developmental stage to benefit most from a program geared to develop her communications skills. If we leave this until later, she may never catch up.

4 March 1992:

Karina is 19 months old. We are putting a lot of effort into teaching her the names of familiar people and the common objects she sees, uses and touches. This is important because children understand words before they can say them.

Play now has more importance to us than I had ever imagined it could have. We must repeat things so often, yet at the same time we need to make learning fun, otherwise we will all get bored and it will fall in a heap.

Make-believe games with a tea set are one of our favourite teaching methods. We are trying to encourage Karina to understand the names of common objects such as a cup and saucer, and to imitate our actions.

Pop-up and wind-up toys are a good way of teaching cause-and-effect. This is important because it is one of the underlying concepts of communication – that is, we say something and there is a result or an effect on our listener.

We are also encouraging Karina to take part in and initiate more social interaction games, such as rolling a ball or toy to another person. She has to learn to make moves, rather than waiting for the world to come to her.

Makaton signs are also now being introduced. Makaton is a simple sign language that uses obvious hand signals for common objects and activities, such as "more", "up", "drink" and "eat".

Because she is now taking a keen interest in watching the movements of others, we need to heighten her awareness of everyday gestures and signs. This way, she might attempt to use them to build on the range of meanings she is already using.

Although Karina can now walk short distances with two hands held, she has poor control and coordination of her lower limbs and her stride length is uneven. She takes quite long strides with her right leg, and the left leg simply follows.

She will now pull herself up on furniture to stand briefly before "plopping" back down on to the floor.

She smiles readily, makes eye contact, claps hands, accepts other people and waves goodbye.

She has settled in well at play group and is now sitting still for longer at story time.

She is now almost weaned and sleeps from 7.30pm until 6am.

26 March 1992:

Karina is much more physically active than she was a few months ago and now plays in a supported standing position.

I am on a sharp learning curve yet again, attempting to help her to learn Makaton signs. It can be frustrating. A simple question like "Would you like a drink, Karina?" means I must first attract her attention, usually by walking over to her and making the sign for drink. At the same time as making the sign, I must repeat the words "Do you want a drink?"

These early stages are frustrating and tiring, because she does not respond consistently. All we are aiming for, at first, is some sort of sound in response. It does not really matter what that sound is — we simply want acknowledgement of our questions, on the understanding that more accurate imitation of our sounds will follow later. This takes a few months.

We are still encouraging Karina to close her mouth rather than ignoring her habit of sitting with her mouth gaping. It is taking time but appears to be paying off.

She has a mild cough and has had a persistent runny nose for several months. She is on the semi-emergency list for grommets for her ears, which we hope will increase her hearing.

2 August 1992:

We celebrated Karina's second birthday with a family party. She sat in her high chair, making a lovely mess of her birthday cake and thoroughly enjoying the attention.

She cannot yet walk unaided, but can walk holding on to our hands. We have been doing this with her for several months now.

15 October 1992:

Two years, two months old. Karina took part in a 45 minute session with the social trainer, changing from one activity to the next about every two to three minutes.

12 December 1992:

Karina can now walk unaided over a short distance. She finds it hard though, and exhausting. She took her first steps without our support about three months ago, at 25 months. It surprises me now that I did not record this fairly major milestone then. Perhaps it was because these first independent steps were so long coming. With most babies it is only a matter of days between the first faltering one or two steps and a preference for upright mobility; with Karina this took much longer. Our sense of *expectation had gone on so long that the edge had been worn off our surprise when it eventually happened.*

Even when she is six, Karina will find it difficult to walk long distances. While her classmates will cover five laps of the school oval, she will manage only three.

But she *does* manage to walk three.

January, 1993:

Rodney and I recently took part in a half-day communication workshop. It emphasised the invaluable role parents and family have to play in helping a child achieve speech.

We have always believed that Karina would learn to speak. She has always seemed, to us, to make a variety of sounds and to respond to speech appropriately. We realise now, however, that the path towards her speech development is going to be a lot slower than we first thought.

If she has the potential to learn speech, then we must run with it. It is her key to social acceptance. With speech she will be able to interact with others in the playground. Without it, she may be isolated.

March, 1993:

Nuffield cards are another part of our speech program. These are picture cards designed to teach the sounds we need to know in order to put the right sounds together to make words. The train card, for instance, is used for the "ch ch ch" sound, a fish with its mouth open for "o", and a candle for the "p" sound, similar to puffing out a candle.

I am delighted to find myself pregnant again. A third child may help shift a little of the focus away from Karina and restore some balance in our family.

7

Another Baby

Rodney and I have been trying for over a year to have another baby, so we are delighted when what I dismiss as a mystery virus turns out to be early signs of pregnancy.

It is early 1993. I finished my Masters thesis last year and am working part-time at a Perth university. Danika is in pre-school and due to move into Year One at our local Montessori school around the middle of the year, and Karina is enjoying her three mornings per week at playgroup there.

We discuss the implications of a third child and both feel that it will complete and balance our family. Whenever we mention to anyone that we are keen to have another child, the general reaction is not one of surprise: "A lot of families with a disabled child tend to have one more" seems to be the general opinion.

Rodney and I are extremely keen for Danika to have another brother or sister. We are already seeing signs of the thoughtful, responsible child that she becomes, and a third child will give her another playmate.

We were also looking to the future, hoping that as an adult Danika will not have to be the only one with family responsibility for Karina, once she is living independently of us. A sibling will, perhaps, be someone with whom Danika can one day share family decision making, celebrations, visits and outings with Karina.

Another child will also take some of the spotlight off Karina. Middle children often suffer from lack of attention, because they are neither the eldest nor the youngest. Karina's gregarious personality gives us confidence that there is little risk of her ever being the family member who is left out — and for a child with a disability, being in the middle can be an advantage. It means they play with and learn from both an older and a younger sibling.

We both realise a new baby will mean more work — though it is not until later that Rodney and I will learn just how much work a new baby can mean with an active Karina at home as well. She is beginning to be quite active when I become pregnant, but the real management nightmare begins the year after Joshua is born. Those two years are the worst ... nothing prepared us for Karina's level of chaotic activity. It seems ironic at times that we had spent so much of her first two years focused on encouraging her to move independently; once she is up and off it is, at times, like living with a small human tornado.

There are of course new considerations with this third pregnancy. We were counselled by a geneticist soon after Karina's birth, and I will be nearly 37 by the time the new baby arrives. I am aware that my chances of having another child with Down Syndrome are increased.

The fact that we have one child with a disability is always at the back of our minds. We do not dwell on it but it is with us. There is no point pretending it is not important.

On the other hand of course, Danika is our proof that we are capable of producing a "normal" child. Perhaps if Karina was our first baby, we would have been less confident about trying for another. It is one of those hypothetical questions, impossible to answer.

Once my pregnancy is confirmed we seek advice about the sorts of tests that are available to us. The Disability Services social trainer puts us in touch with the relevant doctors and psychologists.

After weighing up all the options, we decide to have an amniocentesis at four months. This involves taking a small sample of amniotic fluid and growing the cells to determine the baby's genetic make up. Our decision is based mainly on our need for reassurance. At an early ultrasound the new baby displays every sign of being a boy. He is moving beautifully and does not appear to have Karina's heavy, square bone structure. He appears to have fine features, like a little pixie.

Rodney and I are both quite confident of the outcome, but although the baby appears very active and I am feeling well, I cannot pretend that I enjoy the amniocentesis procedure. It is uncomfortable and I do not like the impersonal, offhand attitude of the person performing the test. I later speak to other women who are treated with the utmost respect and who find the test virtually painless, so I guess this is another area where individual experiences are so different. Much depends on our own expectations and the way we are treated.

Before the pregnancy we had more or less decided that if we tried for another child and tests identified that child as having a disability, we would go ahead with the pregnancy anyway. Rodney says later that to him, a termination would have been like saying to Karina: "You're not perfect; we don't want another one like you."

In truth it is impossible to say what we will do if that is the case. At the back of our minds we know we cannot really make any decision until we have the results ... in the meantime, why torture ourselves worrying about the unknown? We have enough on our hands at this time, and it is another of those very personal issues I believe is impossible to decide — or to judge the decisions of others — until you have been in the situation yourself.

Waiting for results is never easy. Although it is an anxious time for us, we do not really have time to worry unduly. Work and caring for the family keep our minds occupied.

Three weeks later we have the results: a balanced set of chromosomes and definitely a boy. We are over the moon with joy and relief — we do not have to make any difficult decisions. The telephone runs hot as we call our family and friends.

I feel very glad now that I have had the amniocentesis. Knowing the result allows me to move on and enjoy what will almost certainly be my last pregnancy.

Although Karina by this stage has been walking for several months, her mobility is limited and she is still relatively easy to manage. Initially, she gets into very little trouble because she does not have the strength to walk far — ten metres is her limit, before she flops down for a rest. Slopes are totally beyond her, and when she does muster the courage to tackle them, she leans right forward or right back, apparently totally bemused at the way the ground has decided to rise or drop away.

Danika has already started attending a local gymnastics group for juniors, and from mid 1992 I have also been taking Karina along to the toddler group there. She enjoys the contact with other people, and the exercises help build up her arm and leg muscles, encouraging her to develop the coordination she needs to improve her mobility. It fits in with what Danika wants to do, and is fun for all of us.

Karina learns how to do forward rolls at the gym, and her general mobility improves. Sometimes her progress is more readily noticed by the social trainers and physiotherapists, who of course see her less often than we do. To us, Karina's progress always seems slow. It is encouraging to have this source of positive and reliable feedback.

We also believe the strength, grace and poise Danika later develops is helped by her time at the gym. Karina stays in the toddler group until mid 1993, when I am seven months pregnant with Joshua and find it hard physically to manage helping her on the various apparatus. It is time to give it up.

We are also doing a lot of balancing work at home, encouraging Karina to balance and walk along a beam on the ground to help develop her awareness and control (of her body in space). Roadside kerbing is a handy substitute for a balancing beam and we continue to use it to encourage her to straighten her legs when she walks. At this stage we also start to really appreciate the value of local playgrounds, purpose built for the safe development of strength and coordination in young bodies.

Sometimes I have to step back from our situation and see how our focus on directed play must seem to parents of children who do not have a disability. I occasionally must remind myself just to let the children have a bit of their own fun — something that was brought home to me by the comments of a young girl with Down Syndrome, whose mother was conscientiously directing her play to help her develop the skills she needed.

"Oh Mum, I'm enjoying myself. Can't you just let me play!"

Towards the end of the pregnancy I am still carrying Karina more than I would like, but only because she tires so quickly and therefore cannot walk far. People say to me: "You should not be carrying that child", but what else can I do? It is yet another of those situations that seems so easy to judge by people who have not experienced it themselves.

Although I do not dwell on it, I am tired. There are nights when I do not dare sit down to rest because I know that once I do, I will not get up again. Fortunately, I seem to be blessed with good pregnancies so I can keep going without feeling that the baby is at risk. I sometimes describe myself as "a good brood mare".

Rodney and I have discussed the forthcoming birth and plan to use the relatively new birthing centre at King Edward Memorial Hospital. We would like another home birth, but the price is out of our range and we see the birthing centre as a happy compromise. The delivery will take place in surroundings just like home, with expert medical care close at hand if needed.

In the month leading up to Joshua's arrival, I have plenty of what I dismiss as Braxton Hicks contractions. I later wonder whether these false starts to labour remind me of the pain to come, and push my adrenalin level up to a point where the contractions stop. It apparently does not worry me unduly, because when I have the first stronger signs that the baby's arrival is drawing near, I take myself off to the hairdresser and have a perm. Because both my other labours were so long, I am quite confident that Joshua's birth is still some hours away. I notice however that the hairdresser seems a little unnerved.

Later, Rodney and I telephone the birthing centre and drive in for a check-up, which confirms that Joshua is on his way but will most likely be some hours coming. So with the blessing of the midwives, we leave our suitcase at the centre, drive down to one of the hotels we used to go to in the days before we had children, and have a leisurely few games of pool. Then we go shopping and buy each of the girls a new dress, enjoying the luxury of spending time together on our own. Some of the shop assistants seem surprised each time we stop so I can breathe through a new wave of contractions.

We return to the birthing centre in the late afternoon and Joshua is born in the early hours of Wednesday, the 23rd of September.

The three of us return home that evening, collecting the girls from my mother on the way. Rodney has to return to work almost immediately, so within two or three days I am back into the routine of housework and ferrying the girls to and from school and playgroup.

This makes it all sound so straightforward. I just got on with it, but later I will look back and recognise that the days and weeks after Joshua's birth are one of those times when I really should have asked for more outside help. I could do with more support, but I keep going because there is no option.

As Joshua has timed his arrival for the university break, I have one full week at home before I have to return to part-time work for six weeks, until the academic year ends. My mother and one of the carers at the local school look after the baby during the day for the two and a half days I work away from home.

Having a job gives me a break from Karina and our new baby, but it also gives me little chance to recover physically from the pregnancy and delivery. As I am breastfeeding Joshua, and Karina is still waking occasionally, it means I am existing on three to four hours sleep a night. This goes on for 18 months. I recognise that our situation is far from ideal, but accept it because our current financial state makes the extra income necessary.

These 18 months, with Joshua waking through the night and me having to work part-time through the academic year and look after the other children, is the most exhausting of my life. Breastfeeding and my inability to prepare and eat proper meals see my weight drop from 60kg to 54kg. Ironically, on one rare night when Rodney and I go out together for a meal, I cannot finish the food on my plate. I have become so used to snatching snacks where I can that my stomach feels full very quickly. I overeat and suffer for it.

It sometimes feels as though I am literally pushing my body through each day, feeding it as one feeds a car, just to keep it running. Iron tablets and vitamin supplements help. Because of the tiredness (it is only later that I will realise just *how* tired I was) it is difficult to remember events and milestones accurately through this time.

Despite this, we are all very happy. Danika loves school and settles in well when she starts Year Two at St Brigid's, near Midland, early in 1994. The school community is very welcoming and she enjoys this new phase of her life. Karina is walking and starting to make real progress in other areas, and we have a beautiful new baby boy. The unconditional love our children give us more than makes up for the hard time we are going through.

It is around this time that we have regular contact with a social trainer who is sensitive not only to Karina's needs, but to mine as well. She recognises we could do with some help and organises for us to reestablish contact with support groups, including Activ Foundation and Community Support Services.

We have been members of Activ Foundation before, but when our finances became limited we let our memberships of various organisations lapse. And although we have already given the Foundation's respite care service a trial, it did not work out. The carer and I had a difference of opinion, but I wish I had had the confidence then to persist with another carer. Instead, we gave up and my mother stepped in to help.

Now we rejoin the Foundation and start to use the respite service again, this time successfully. Community Support Services help by subsidising the cost of a fortnightly cleaner. It is like a breath of fresh air to come home once a fortnight to a clean house, as I have virtually given up on all but the basic housework.

Karina loves her new brother — to the extent that I cannot trust her with him. She tries to pick him up and carry him at every opportunity.

The upshot of all this is that during the first year I carry Joshua everywhere with me when both children are awake. I become skilled at doing the laundry, hanging out nappies, washing dishes and preparing meals with one hand. If I need to go to the toilet, I lay Joshua on a towel on the floor and hold onto Karina, diverting her with a story.

It is only safe to put Joshua down when she is asleep, or when I sit down and play with both children. Again some people tell me "you are making a rod for your own back, carrying that child all the time. You'll make him clingy". And again, what else can I do? One of my critics does admit later that she was wrong; while Joshua is quite clingy for a while, he later becomes as independent as any other three year old. I believe carrying him is for his safety, not because I feel insecure.

Showering at night through this time means first sorting clothes for the three children and myself and placing them in heaps, then placing both Danika and Karina in the bath under the shower, undressing Joshua, washing him, wrapping him in a towel, and laying him on our clothes while I get into the bath with the girls. Then, in turn, I quickly dry and dress myself, Joshua and Karina, and help Danika get ready for bed.

The school run also turns into a weight-lifting exercise, as I have to carry Joshua and Karina with me each morning and afternoon when I escort Danika to her classroom. At three and a half, Karina is nearing the peak of her "walk and flop" stage, which means it is easier to carry her (although she is getting heavy).

Towards the middle of the year, she achieves another milestone. She trots away from me and keeps going, further than I anticipate. With Joshua tucked under one arm, I have to sprint across the oval after her. All our work to get her to move is starting to pay off.

By the summer of 1994, both Karina and Joshua are on the move. I have two toddlers and management becomes a little harder; I know I have to put Joshua down more to allow him to learn to play and do things for himself. I have to be particularly vigilant when they are awake simultaneously. I work around their sleep times.

Karina is now starting to become more independent of me, and more assertive about her likes and dislikes. Behaviour management is our big challenge — sticking to our rules (the rules of the house) is our priority whenever there is a battle of wits. We do not expect too much of

Karina, but we do try to be firm, keeping the rules simple, clear and consistent. Being human, we often fail. Keeping up with her whirlwind personality when she is in full flight is very, very wearing.

We become hardened to questioning looks from people who are apparently wondering why we are not doing more to keep our daughter in check. Others dismiss her actions as those of a "typical toddler". They are right, but with most children the typical toddler behaviour peaks at around two or three years of age, then gradually matures. With Karina, everything will take much longer. Scooping up a screaming two year old in the middle of a shopping centre is hard enough, but trying to manage a strong and active four or five year old in the same situation will be a lot harder.

One of the worse aspects of child behaviour management for parents is how it looks to other people, particularly when the child has a disability. When I attempt to put her in a shopping trolley, there are protests. It is not that I am hurting her, of course, but simply that she is quite happy in her stroller and resists the change. As fast as I get her right foot through the gap at the front of the trolley, she will have her left foot out. She struggles, I struggle, and when the trolley starts to move off, she screams at the top of her voice. Within five minutes she is happily settled, but meanwhile her screams get others' attention – and it does not look good.

In situations like this it is always a tremendous help when another shopper offers to hold the trolley until she is settled. Little acts like these make such a big difference.

Even when she is older, Karina's behaviour will be hard on her siblings sometimes. She will continue to learn to "play the game" at home, and at times this causes tension, particularly for Danika. Although we like our children to have an opportunity to develop some sense of responsibility, we want them to enjoy their childhood too, and it saddens me when I think she is assuming too much responsibility simply because she happens to have a sibling who often does not know when to stop.

An example is when Danika spends 20 minutes making a play "horse" from a picnic table and household items for her younger sister and brother to play on with her. Karina adores Danika, and is always delighted to be invited to share in her games. All too often, however, her excitement spills over into the sort of wild behaviour that sabotages the success of the game. This time she constantly interrupts Danika as she tries to make the horse, until eventually I have to remove her so her sister can finish it. Later, when all three children are having their ride, Karina keeps rocking the table until, for the sake of safety, the game is ended. By this stage, Danika is understandably at screaming point.

Before having children I learned meditation and the importance of focusing on my breathing as an aid to relaxation. There are many times in the early years when these relaxation techniques prove useful. When diversion fails, I whistle or hum, and have also learned to take advantage of the rare moments I get to myself. In the time it takes to walk the 10 or 12 steps from the rear side passenger door (after securing Karina in her car seat) to the driver's door, for example, I consciously slow my breathing. This "slows the world down", otherwise we all get too wound up. It is important to make the most of such brief snatches of time.

Throughout 1994 we make a big effort to encourage Karina to learn to use a potty. At home we keep her out of nappies during the day, to try to help her make the connection. We are supported in this by staff at Midland Occasional Care Centre, where Karina and Joshua stay when I have to work. Staff there are wonderful, also helping to reinforce the sounds and Makaton signs Karina is learning.

We aim to have her out of nappies by 1995, when she is due to start pre-school.

8

Karina Starts School

We realised quite early that one must be able to manage a child's behaviour before that child can be educated. Social skills are equally important, and the child who runs around the classroom, hits other children and refuses to sit down and listen does not find school easy and makes it hard for others in the class. When a child has a disability, behaviour management and the development of appropriate social skills can be challenging.

As we have always been keen for Karina to have the opportunity for education in the wider community, it is a challenge we start working at from an early age. From the time she was a few weeks old, we began preparing her to feel comfortable in situations where she has to behave with other children.

The visits from the Disability Services social trainers are Karina's introduction to such situations. Eventually, she will be expected to sit still, listen and follow simple instructions.

There are many times when her behaviour, particularly at sessions conducted in an environment away from home, is best described as "chaotic", but we stick at it. We persevere where parental embarrassment might otherwise drive us away, and we believe that approach pays off. We learn that Karina will settle down, eventually, once a new learning environment becomes familiar to her. Although it sometimes seems she is too distracted to learn anything at some of the sessions, there are times when her subsequent behaviour proves this to be wrong.

Karina started going to day-care quite early, partly because I had to work, but also to provide her with plenty of contact with other children. We want her to feel comfortable as part of a group.

I begin enquiring about her education options early in 1994, when she is three and a half. Midway through that year, Rodney and I attend a meeting organised by Disability Services with parents of children due to start school the following year. We discuss what is available — essentially we have the choice of a special school, a school with a special unit for children with disabilities, or integrating her into the State or private school system.

Integration is our first choice. We have always hoped that Karina will one day take her place in the real community, and believe the nature of her disability makes this possible. Children and adults with some other types of disability may be better off in a segregated educational setting, but we do not think this will be appropriate for Karina.

We are keen to enrol her at St Brigid's Catholic Primary School, in Middle Swan. Danika is very happy there, and we like the warm sense of community the school provides. But will they take Karina?

Our initial inquiries are promising so, with support from Disability Services, we enrol her at St Brigid's at the end of 1994, to start pre-school in 1995. As a back up, we also enrol her at another school that has a special unit for children with disabilities.

By this stage, Karina is starting to use the toilet. She is cooperative, outgoing, likes books, and is starting to sit down and listen. She is quite content sitting in a circle with other children to eat a piece of fruit or lunch, and can also hold a pen, look through a book, and has been gluing since she was three.

Later I realise it was unfortunate that I did not place more emphasis on these positive achievements. When Rodney and I, along with a representative from Disability Services, meet with school staff late in 1994, to give them a better idea of Karina's specific needs, I instead begin launching into my well prepared list of the things she can't do. I mention what she can do, but deliver the "bad news" first. Toileting, which (like everything else) took a lot longer to achieve than we once hoped, is the biggest concern at this stage. Although I mention it, I later regret not placing more emphasis on her wonderful personality. Karina might have her problems, but she is considered an asset by staff with every program she has been involved in so far. She always contributes positively to any social group, through sheer charisma and her genuine love of people.

As well as our little group, the headmaster, deputy headmaster, two pre-primary teachers, a special school coordinator and a special aide, are in the room. Karina is very excited at being the centre of attention, and behaves accordingly. She greets people, interrupts when staff are talking, explores the contents of boxes and shelves, and rearranges whatever takes her fancy. I am worried that our interview is not going well; as her mother, I am being oversensitive. I want the staff to be happy about having Karina as part of the school — not to feel she is a chore they have to accept.

It is comforting later to hear one of the pre-primary teachers say many children of Karina's age would behave similarly in a new and stimulating environment, whether or not they have a disability. The same teacher says she is prepared to have Karina in her class in 1995.

The importance of that meeting stands out to me more later than it did at that the time. The lines of communication have been opened, but most importantly, everyone has a chance to meet Karina. Her behaviour has not been ideal, but it has been seen.

Early in 1995, she starts attending two mornings a week. This continues until late in the first term, when her mornings increase to three for Term Two and most of Term Three. Her time increases to two half days and one full day, and towards the end of Term Four, she goes on to two full days and one half day a week.

This gradual introduction to pre-school suits Karina, who initially finds school hard work, and later, still finds it tiring. The schedule fits around the aide time the school has been allotted. A special aide works with Karina each morning, and in the afternoons, she manages without this assistance, thanks partly to the wonderful work of her teacher and teacher's aide. Her education time, now and in the future, depends on the availability of funding to pay for the time of a special aide to help her work at her own program within the class.

I cannot pretend that the first few weeks are easy for any of us. It is a time of enormous transition for me and I shed more than a few tears on that important first day. Having been through the process of starting to "let go" of Danika, when she began school, it is not unexpected, but it is still hard. For four and a half years I have been the pivot of Karina's life. With our visits from social trainers, the emphasis has always been on me telling them what Karina can and can't do ... now, suddenly, I am the one having to listen. It is not for me to tell her teacher what to do.

Taking the back seat can be hard, particularly when your child is involved — and more particularly when your child has a disability. Hard as it is, though, I acknowledge the importance of good communication. Arguing seldom helps anyone, least of all the child who may be the subject of that argument.

The pre-school teacher who has agreed to have Karina in her class has been teaching more than 20 years, but has never taught a child with Down Syndrome. I am well aware that this will be a new experience for her — she will be learning as well. She has to get to know Karina, has to find out what teaching her will be like, and has to put in place a program to suit her needs. I appreciate her tremendously for her willingness to take on my daughter, and try to stand back at the start, while they get used to each other.

I am also aware from the beginning that Karina's disability means there will be a lot more problem solving ahead than would be the case if she had not been born with Down Syndrome. Therefore, if we are to get anywhere, it is important to have a spirit of cooperation, and I believe this is important with all our children. We always try to listen to the teacher, to help in the classroom when asked, and to mention when things seem to be going well or badly.

Karina's teacher and I do not always agree. She is very direct, and says exactly what she thinks; there are times when I do not know how to take her, so things can be a little uneasy while we are establishing our teacher/mother relationship. What is important is that we keep talking, and are both willing to learn from each other.

After a few weeks, we begin using what we call a Communication Book. This is an exercise book in which each of us writes down relevant messages about Karina's achievements, any problems either of us might be having with her, work suggestions, and appointment times. This works in two ways. It keeps the lines of communication open in a positive and cooperative way, and means I am not monopolising the teacher's time each morning and afternoon when all the children are arriving and departing with their parents.

Karina enjoys pre-school once she settles in. Her behaviour is, as expected, quite chaotic at times throughout the first term. She is still learning and adjusting to a new routine, and most mornings will run to the bookshelves, or one of the bright and attractive displays, almost as though she is asking: "What do I do?". Her special aide is there to help her keep on track, and once she learns what is expected of her, life becomes a lot easier for everyone. She has always enjoyed a familiar routine, so we are not surprised that the orderliness of the school environment suits her.

While we are delighted with her progress during 1995, at the end of her first year we agree with her teacher that she would benefit from a little more of the same in 1996. She begins full-time pre-school in Term Two, 1996, and goes on to develop skills in listening, writing and cutting, as well as her social skills.

We learn that Karina will be going on to Year One in 1997, and I am surprised just how thrilled we are when she comes home with the Year One equipment list, just like everyone else. It has taken six years to get her here.

Next year she will have her own program within the Year One framework. When the class is writing she will be writing too, but will be working within this individual program. A special aide will be there to help her in the classroom.

The move to Year One will also mark the end of our involvement with the Early Intervention Program. Just over one year ago I felt apprehensive when we began to be eased away from the program that has helped Karina to do so much, and has taught us so many things that we can do to help her. As it happens, this easing away has been so gradual that we are quite confident as we move on to encourage and follow her future development through the school system.

9

What About Dad?

By coincidence, Rodney Potter had some involvement with people with Down Syndrome before Karina was born. For twelve months he was chairman of the West Australian committee of the Citizen Youth Award, a program run by the international Hoo Hoo Club, a service organisation of people involved in the wood working industry. Its annual youth awards program is designed to encourage and recognise the work of young people with a range of physical and intellectual disabilities, who work with wood.

Rodney could not have known then that four years later his second daughter would be born with Down Syndrome. Here he shares some of his experiences in the past six years and his thoughts about Karina and her disability...

Before becoming involved with the Citizen Youth Award, I had wondered what it would be like to work with people with a disability such as Down Syndrome, and had been apprehensive. Then I volunteered and was thrown in the deep end, having to tie it all together, visit schools and promote the award, and help a lot of the participants with their models.

I found I got along well with the people with Down Syndrome, because they were so happy, easygoing, outgoing and friendly. Everyone who took part in the program was awarded a trophy or certificate and the most magic thing about it all was that many of these kids had never been recognised before for anything they had done.

Had I known in the days after Karina's birth (when we first heard the diagnosis) that she would be the little girl she is today, I would not have worried so much, but back then Gun and I knew so little, and we wanted answers to so much.

Karina's birth was pretty much as I had expected. What sticks in my mind most is Jill wanting to move things along near the end, and Gun wanting to bite down on my hand! Apart from that it all seemed straightforward, very natural and peaceful. We were at home, there was no intervention, everything was happening as Nature had intended. My mother and father were there looking after Danika. With the family around it was very pleasant and laid back.

Shortly after Karina was born I had a feeling that something was not right. It is difficult to explain but I have these feelings sometimes, like a premonition, and now I am learning to go with them. I dismissed it then, however, because by that stage Gun and I were both so tired, and I was busy showing off Karina and getting the champagne. Even later when Jill and my mother took Karina to the hospital, we did not think anything of it. It seemed to us to be a good idea to give the baby a check up, just a normal precaution, and it never crossed my mind that there might be something wrong. Looking back it seems it would have been strange if we had thought that.

The morning after Karina's birth, when Gun and I were preparing to go to the hospital, my mother gave me a hug. She seemed terribly upset and her behaviour puzzled me. I did not know whether it was just pure joy or what, but as emotions tend to run amok around a birth, I did not think too much about it. I was still on a high because I had a brand new daughter and was looking forward to going in to the hospital to see her.

At the hospital it was a shock to see Karina in the humidicrib, connected to tubes. Obviously then I realised something was wrong, and the feeling of dread and unease that I had had just after the birth came back. Even then it did not cross my mind that she might have some sort of disability – I simply could not work out why our poor baby was like that.

The hardest part was waiting to see the paediatrician, with Karina in the humidicrib beside us. When the paediatrician said he was 95 per cent sure she had been born with Down Syndrome, it took a couple of hours for it to start to sink in. The worst thing then was that we knew so little about what it all meant for Karina and for us. The doctors and nurses explained what Down Syndrome meant, but at that stage no-one could really give us the answers we wanted. We had all sorts of questions about learning difficulties and life expectancy ... our little baby was lying there, and we wondered if that was how she would be forever.

The hospital staff were wonderful but they could only give us support for the condition as they saw it, which is why they introduced us to the Down Syndrome Association. It was a relief, later, when we met a family with a Down Syndrome child – a child running around doing what normal children do.

The hardest thing for me was hearing that the life expectancy of a person with this disability was around 40 years. We now know that to be an underestimate, but at that stage all we really knew was that our child had been born with Down Syndrome and she had a shortened life expectancy. It was as though we were living in a nightmare: why had this happened to me? Poor, poor me. Poor pity her.

We stayed at the hospital that first night and came home so physically and emotionally drained. Karina was our child and we loved her dearly — we had to come to terms with what it all meant, but when you have a child you expect it to grow up, go to school, get a job, find a partner and have children ... to go through life in the normal way. What was the reality of our situation now?

Everyone has their own grief. My mother was incredibly upset and we were all trying to comfort one another. Family is not like friends. Our parents were grieving in the way that one does as a parent — when your own child is upset it is twice the tragedy. My mother could not tell us how she felt, so she wrote me a note the morning we were at the hospital and gave it to me the next day.

Just how much of a handicap would Down Syndrome be for Karina? Did it mean she would not be able to go to school? Would she be with us for the rest of her life, or one day live independently? We craved information and were bombarded with it; it was hard to keep up with it while coming to terms with the situation. The main message was that there were organisations available to help us.

When I had to return to work, it was Gun who had to deal with all the new information. She always told me what was happening, which made it easier, because I could not always be there at medical appointments and when the Early Intervention Program visits started. Gun has a tendency to overdescribe things by repeating them, as much to reinforce them in her own mind as mine, and this has proved to be a great advantage.

The Early Intervention Program has been invaluable. Without it, Karina would not have developed the skills she needs to cope with day-care and school as early as she did, or the chance to develop her personal communication skills.

Because it has the various stages of child development so well set out, we could see that Karina was making progress once she started achieving each stage. This in itself was incentive to carry on.

It was impossible, in those early days, to predict what the future held, and while the same is true now, there is not that level of anxiety. Karina will soon be starting to learn self-care skills, and when she was tested recently to assess her aptitude for the program, she amazed me with her ability to reason. I believe she could learn quite readily if she could hear and talk.

Communication is the hardest thing, and can be frustrating for her and those around her. A good example of this happened recently in the school car park, when she did not want to walk with me and threw a tantrum. She would usually rather be carried than walk, but she is too heavy now and I often have to crouch down in front of her, establish positive eye contact, and encourage her to walk with me. When I do carry her I make sure the ride is not too comfortable, and while she walks I make sure to offer her plenty of reassurance and encouragement. On this particular day, I had wrongly assumed her frustration at being made to walk stemmed from her wanting to be carried, but in fact she *did* want to walk — with her sister and brother, not her father.

When I was six or seven I found it very hard to talk to people. My shyness and inability to communicate were so bad that I was referred to a clinic in West Perth for treatment. This brought me out of myself, so I can empathise with Karina. I know how it feels, and to be made fun of because of it.

As a father I am protective of my three children, but especially of Karina. When I hear that a disabled person has been intentionally hurt I get angry, and extremely self-righteous and upset when I hear that the government is cutting funds to the disabled. I feel as though the treatment has been personally directed at my daughter.

The idea of her being looked after in our own home, with Danika and Joshua, so Gun and I can have the occasional respite weekend does not worry me ... but I do not like the idea of Karina going into weekend care with another family at all. Even though I can see it could be good for the rest of us, it feels to me as though we would be giving her away to someone else to look after, as if we would be saying "we don't want you this weekend". I would feel as though I had failed her.

It angers and hurts me when other children treat her as a curiosity. The children who know Karina are very protective of her, but sometimes other children take the mickey and use her as the butt of their jokes. She will still be laughing, even though they are pushing her over and starting to hurt her, because she wants to be part of the game.

It also hurts sometimes when I see her now with her own siblings, trying to play at their level. Recently she spent a lot of time and effort putting a rope around the table legs to make a corral so she could join in a game of "horses". By the time she had finished the other two had moved on to something else. I don't blame them — this is just one of the new stages we are at now.

All Karina really wants is to be accepted, to fit in. At school there is a strict regime and she knows exactly what to expect. At lunch time, for instance, the children sit down in a circle, open their lunch boxes, unwrap their lunch and eat it, then put their scraps in the bin and the lids back on their lunch boxes. It is all very ordered and Karina performs extraordinarily well. At home she is a real larrikin, fighting with Joshua and misbehaving.

I see our other two children more likely to grow up and be in a normal life situation. Karina has now reached the stage where her personality and natural magnetism are going to be far outweighed by what she can achieve. She has to be able to perform to a certain level for her life skills, and we will not know what she can achieve from life until she actually achieves it.

The path of Karina's life is uncertain, and although it does not worry her in the least, as parents we are protective and want the best for her. I am very proud of her and of what she can do, given the disability she has.

10

Let's Party

Children's birthday parties are dangerous ground for parents. Weeks of planning, preparation and agonising over guest lists can result in a roaring success — or a roaring flop.

Karina's party, the day after her sixth birthday, can only be described as an overwhelming success. The love shown by the children and their parents towards her, and her own joy and pride in being the perfect hostess, resolves some of the worries we have about her part in the school community.

We celebrate each of our children's birthdays every year; we believe parties are important to help teach the value of friendship to children ... childhood is so fleeting. For Karina in particular, this is an opportunity to thank her network of friends, and it lets other people see that she can enjoy a regular birthday party just like any other child.

It is the best present anyone could give her. She loves people, and the noise, warmth and activity that goes with them.

Choosing a conventional present for her has never been easy. We put a lot of thought into our choice of gift: a push-button viewer that projects pictures from a magazine of frames onto a wall. Many toys and games are not appropriate for her because they rely upon the imagination of the child using them, and Karina's play is seldom creative. She loves television and videos, but we want to give her something a little more challenging, something that will encourage her to do things for herself. The viewer requires her to push a button to move a new picture on to the wall, and I often hear her conducting a "pishesho" (picture show) for Joshua in the hallway. She is in charge, and loves it.

For the big event, I book a party room at our local McDonald's Family Restaurant in Midland. McDonald's has become one of our favourite places, for a number of reasons. It has a safe, enclosed play area, the food is reasonably priced and if I provide the children with a plate of fruit when they get home, I can be confident they have had a balanced meal.

Most important for us though is the consideration and tolerance of McDonald's staff for chaotic children with disabilities. It is not unusual for Karina to run across the kitchen to the drive-through servery window and start handing out serviettes to people in their cars before we can catch up with her. She eagerly talks to the cashiers, and though this would cause embarrassment in many places, at McDonald's there is minimal fuss.

When making the booking, I mention her disability and ask, if possible, for someone who has experience with active children like Karina to be assigned to our function. I also suggest it might be a good idea if a second person is assigned, and the management could not be more helpful, even organising staff to swap rosters to accommodate our booking.

Earlier, I ask Karina's teachers for the names of six children in the pre-primary school who have spent time with her and who include her in their play. With other friends, the party grows to 15 children on the day. Some are from Year One, children who knew her in pre-school last year.

Because she is a boisterous, active child, she tends to play more with boys than with girls her own age. She attracts the active, caring boys and the "mothering" five and six year old girls. Girls who play quietly in select groups seldom have the patience for a child like Karina. She does, however, tend to bring out the best from often unexpected sources.

Last year, for example, one of her allies was a boy who was often in trouble — just minor misdemeanours, the sort for which small boys are notorious — yet towards Karina he was extremely protective and took the time to include her in his play. For this he was deservedly praised. She had brought out a side of his nature that might not otherwise have been revealed. We are delighted when she is invited to his birthday party.

Party Saturday begins as usual at 5.30am with Karina climbing the stairs to the main bedroom and flinging herself heavily between Rodney and I for a cuddle and chat before a quick sleep. We have perfected the lightning roll-apart, because woe betide the one who is in the middle of the bed when her bottom hits the sheets.

At breakfast, she asks for "tote" (toast), using the Makaton sign for bread or a sandwich, and "bababa" (her word for milk). Yet again we correct her.

"You mean you want 'milk' Karina?"

She butters her own toast and folds it into a sandwich.

After breakfast we all go grocery shopping. These days, when I have the three children on my own, I avoid this chore — and avoid it at all costs with Karina and Joshua together. A sometimes chaotic six year old and an active boy toddler can be an explosive combination.

Karina is my first choice if I must take one child and I am not in a rush. She enjoys the interaction with people and, being surrounded by things that are new to her, is more easily distracted than either Danika or Joshua. Because she is not possessive of things, there are no demands. As long as I have the time to keep talking to her and maintain her interest, she is quite easy to manage and remains happy and cooperative.

A year ago it was a totally different story. One of her worst habits was flopping down and refusing to walk, so that I often had to pick her up and carry her to the car. At that stage I worried how I was going to manage her and Joshua both, once she grew too big to carry. Trying to get safely from the car to the shopping centre with one child was hard enough, but with the two of them together it was a real struggle.

Around this time, Disability Services suggested I apply for an ACROD sticker. It would be safer and easier for all of us if our car was as near as possible to the kerb and shopping centre entrance, but our application was not successful. Karina was not considered sufficiently physically disabled to justify us having access to an ACROD bay. If more shopping centre managers took the initiative and made available (upon application) such marked bays to regular customers, the weekly battle with strollers, babies and toddlers — and children like Karina — would be much easier.

These days I avoid places where she is likely to have to walk further than I can expect of her. When she does sit down and wants to be carried, I try to encourage her to walk, even if it means that she walks on my feet with me holding her chest.

Now, it is time to get ready for the party. It is difficult to say whether Karina is looking forward to it — she knows we are going to McDonald's, because when I asked her about her party she says "Dododo (McDonald's) ... my ... Ina" with gestures indicating a party. She does not always show excitement about an event in advance and I am not sure whether she can anticipate, based on her recollection of previous events. It is one of the questions I hope to ask her when she is able to talk more clearly.

Certainly she is pleased with herself when she dresses up in her skirt, stockings and jumper. By now both Danika and Joshua are also excited.

We arrive at McDonald's at 2.45pm, to give the helpers an opportunity to meet Karina before her friends and their parents begin arriving. I am overwhelmed by the affection shown to her, but undoubtedly the biggest thrill for me is the way she greets each of her guests with a big hug and a "ta tu" (thank you) as they hand her their presents.

Later, when the ice-cream cake is brought out, she sits perfectly still while everyone sings *Happy Birthday*, waiting until the song is almost finished before blowing out the candles in two big breaths. A year ago she would not have had the patience.

The whole party has been a revelation, in many ways. It is busy, but what party of 15 five and six year old children isn't? Perhaps I have grown used to chaos, but I genuinely expected more. Karina's behaviour has been exemplary.

•

Activ Foundation is looking for a host family to take Karina for one weekend each month, and she will soon be able to join events such as residential weekends at Landsdale Farm School, near Perth. This will give Rodney and I some time with Danika and Joshua on their own, and we are also considering enrolling them in some sibling workshops, run through the Foundation.

A lot of work lies ahead, but life generally is getting easier for us now, as Karina has more awareness of boundaries and more respect for them. When I say "Now we go to the car", the chance that she will actually move towards the car is higher. She is able to follow through an instruction, and is not so easily distracted. Her self-control is better, her social skills more refined, and she is able to communicate better, in her own way. She is changing from a chaotic toddler to a fun-loving young girl.

Karina has begun to recognise by sight some of the words that are important to her. She can select her favourite video tape, for example, from the word "Bambi" written on the jacket, even though there is no picture of a deer to prompt her. She has also begun drawing pictures of people, with eyes, hair, legs and a mouth, giving us confidence that she can eventually develop the skills necessary to write.

Three months ago her attempts to write her own name resulted in a series of crosses. Now there is more form, as her hand/eye coordination and pen control have improved. She enjoys trying to print, and those of us who know her, recognise her series of symbols — the beginnings of a "K" that is always at the start of her name, and the downstroke/dot of an "i", which she performs with great flourish. She also recently completed the drawing of a car, which Rodney had started, adding hair, eyes, nose and a mouth to "Osha" (Joshua), the figure behind the wheel. All this tells us that she is starting to see word and picture patterns, and is beginning to reproduce them from memory. This in turn tells us she has the capacity to learn written language.

Speech is one of our biggest challenges just now, because Karina's speech development has reached a critical stage. Comparisons can be dangerous, but I cannot help noticing that Joshua (at nearly three) has passed the current stage of Karina's speech

Most children learning to speak will know far more words than they are able to say. With Karina, this is exaggerated. Although she can only verbalise at around the 18 months' level, she understands the meaning of many more words than a child at that age. Her speech is a poor reflection of both her level of comprehension and her social skills, which can be confusing to people who do not know her. Speech is one of the obvious cues we use to assess a child's maturity, and they assume, from her limited speech, that she understands far less than she does.

Not knowing when Karina is going to reach a particular milestone is one of the problems we have had to try to overcome, because we need to recognise each new developmental stage in order to make the most of it. Having had Danika, I have some idea of the changes to look out for in Karina's speech development, but it has been difficult at times because nothing is predictable when a child has a disability. The monitoring goes on and on, sometimes for years.

This is another area where the experience of Disability Services staff has been invaluable. Karina has regularly attended speech therapy groups over the past three years and a speech therapist is also visiting us at home each week. Work on Karina's speech now occupies around 80 per cent of the time we spend working with her; she is receptive, and we are capitalising on her interest to the full.

Although we are confident she will eventually learn to speak, her speech will probably always be muffled. Speech involves a high degree of coordination, which makes it particularly hard for her. This is why it is important for us to continue encouraging her to use Makaton signs to help her communicate. She may always need to supplement her speech with signs.

She ably demonstrated this to me recently when she raced in to report some big news from the backyard, where she had been playing with our huge new puppy. The only words I could understand were "dod" (dog) and a guttural "chchch" sound (her sound for bang or crash) accompanied by a startled expression. I had some idea what had happened, but pretended not to, to see if she would work a little harder at getting her message across. After repeating the original message, she eventually flung herself backwards on to the floor. It was a very creative demonstration of a small child being knocked flying by a dog, and the most vivid evidence yet that she has the ability to learn to communicate — even though her methods may not be conventional.

Last term at pre-school, she was presented with a merit certificate for putting on her own shoes. This represented no small victory for her and for the teachers, parents and pupils who for most of the year have refused to be coerced into doing it for her. Early in the year the teachers helped all the pre-schoolers to put on their shoes, and Karina found this such an acceptable arrangement that she continued to badger anyone she could to do it for her, well after the other pupils had been left to learn to manage alone. Eventually, her helpers began to politely refuse, and

85

she tired of thrusting her shoes into their faces, deciding it was easier to do it herself.

Saying "no" to a child with a disability is not easy. But while the average child can take weeks or months to break a bad habit, a child with a disability can take much longer.

She was awarded her second merit certificate at school assembly last week, for being independent (of her special aide) at activity time in the classroom. We are delighted with her award, as it shows she is beginning to understand how to "play the game" and work with the people around her.

Just as significant to us was her behaviour at the presentation ceremony. After several mock presentations at home the previous evening and early that morning, Karina quickly stood up when her name was called, made her way to the dais, accepted her certificate and shook her teacher's hand. Then, after some gentle direction towards the back of the dais, she took her place with the other awardees and remained standing quietly in the group for 10 minutes, until the assembly ended.

•

When I look back now at the letter I wrote to my friends soon after Karina was born — the letter that was never posted — I see how naive I was. It reflects my desperate attempt to come to grips with an overwhelming amount of new and important information all at once, and reads almost as if I thought that by learning as much as I could about Down Syndrome, I would be a better mother to

Karina. It was my way of starting to learn to live with trauma.

Now I see that I chose to deal with my grief in a very detached way.

Six years on, we have learned how valuable the knowledge and experience of others has been in helping Karina's development so far. Being part of the early intervention program, for example, has helped us to help her develop skills she might not otherwise have achieved, certainly not at the same rate. It has meant that wherever possible we have been prompting Karina in the direction most appropriate to her stage of learning, at the critical time, and has also provided us with invaluable support, as her teachers and as her family.

As she reaches each new developmental stage, our learning curve sharpens again as we learn what we need to do to nudge her towards the skills that will bring her a better quality of life. This will continue for a long time, but these days the desperation evident in my letter has gone. Karina has taught us the value of patience, persistence, and the important things in life.

Six years ago when people recognised her as a baby with Down Syndrome, and told us how lucky we were, I genuinely believed they were only saying it to make us feel better. Now I know they were right. Karina is the one person in our family who always wakes up happy and stays that way through most of the day. She is completely happy just being herself, enjoying life.

Parents of older children with a disability may read this and consider us to be naive about the challenges that now lie ahead ... but perhaps a lack of knowledge can be an advantage occasionally? It at least leaves us with the optimism to face those challenges with an open mind.

Often in the wider community there is the misconception that children born with Down Syndrome share the same disabilities and developmental problems. Their physical features give them a commonality, as though they belong to the one family. This apparent sameness is misleading, for just as every child is an individual, every child with Down Syndrome is an individual too. The degree of disability and learning potential varies enormously.

This is our story of Karina's development and the impact her first six years have had on our lives. Because every child with Down Syndrome is different, every child's story will be different, but we hope there is something in Karina's to help other parents and carers of children with special needs.

•

8 June 1998:

Karina has just returned from a weekend camp with four other children with disabilities and a group of carers. It was organised by Kids Camps, an organisation that provides respite care for families like us.

It was her first weekend away from us, and the serenity was palpable! I could not help noticing, as we waited for her to get off the camp bus, how worn the carers looked (do we ever look that tired?). One woman was limping, having twisted her ankle while trying to keep pace with a particularly active boy.

This time has been a marvellous revelation for me. Danika and Joshua played with Danika's favourite Lego, chemistry set and puzzles, calmly and cooperatively. We went for walks, played with the children, and threw ourselves into gardening as a family. On Saturday evening we all went out to dinner and ate in peace while carrying on small talk — one of the casualties of the fraught lifestyle we have come to accept.

I was able to hang out washing, clean the house, go to the toilet, shower, read the weekend papers and eat meals without constantly checking to make sure someone knew where Karina was and what she was doing. The tight feelings in my gut, the paranoia and straining ears had a holiday too this weekend.

We love Karina dearly and she adds something wonderful to our lives, but sometimes I cannot help feeling jealous of families who do not have a child like her. I suggest to Rodney, tongue-in-cheek, that perhaps we were unwise to send her to camp — now we know what we have been missing!

We will of course continue as we are, but this past weekend has shown us that maybe we need to use the respite services such as Kids Camps more often. Then we can arrange family outings and activities that are suitable for Danika and Joshua — and when we are all together, we will value and enjoy each other's company more.

2 August 1998

A busy week. Three days after Karina's eighth birthday party we learn she has been provisionally diagnosed as having Attention Deficit Hyperactivity Disorder (ADHD). Her behaviour is typical of a Type 1 child – easily distracted, fidgety, impulsive, under achieving, frequently disruptive and hyperactive in most situations.

The paediatrician assessing Karina's behaviour describes children with this type of ADHD as being like "a bull in a china shop" and I cannot help but agree with him. It is an expression I have used many times myself to describe her chaotic behaviour.

Again we are facing the unknown. What will this new diagnosis mean and how will it affect our lives?

But besides the uncertainty, there is also tremendous relief. When a child behaves as Karina often does, parents can feel guilty: Is my parenting inefficient? Not all children with Down Syndrome behave as Karina does. Here we have a possible explanation.

Her behaviour will be reassessed in a few months, after we have had time to consider the management options available to us. Then we will start another round of working with health professionals and others involved in Karina's welfare to try to do what is best for her.

Glossary

Activ Foundation   a family-based, non-profit organisation creating accommodation, employment and recreational opportunities for people with developmental disability.

Apgar Score   measures (via heart rate, breathing, skin colour and responses) how quickly a newborn baby is adapting to its environment outside the mother. The test, rated on a scale of zero to 10, is done at one minute after birth, and repeated at five minutes.

Developmental Assessment Record   a detailed scale used during the time Karina was taking part in the Early Intervention Program. It assessed fine and gross motor development, receptive and expressive language, cognitive development, self-help skills, socialisation and play.

Let-down Reflex   the milk ejection reflex that happens in response to hormones released in the mother when her baby starts sucking on the breast.

Feldenkrais   a method of movement said to
                               stimulate development. Prompts
                               people of all ages and abilities to
                               continue learning more efficient,
                               easier ways of moving.

Reflexology   a gentle form of healing done by
                               applying alternating pressure to
                               reflex points on the hands, feet or
                               ears, which correspond to the
                               organs of the body.

Trisomy 21   someone with an extra Number 21
                               chromosome, or part thereof, as
                               well as the existing pair.

Resources

Down Syndrome

Down's Syndrome Association
155 Mitcham Road
London SW17 9PG
Tel: 0181 682 4001 Fax: 0181 682 4012
E-mail: downs-syndrome.org.uk
Provides a comprehensive information and support network and publishes a quarterly newsletter, as well as leaflets and a mail-order book list.

Down Syndrome Association
5 Fitzwilliam Place
Dublin 2
Ireland
Tel: 0035 31 676 9255

Down's Ed: The Down's Syndrome Educational Trust
The Sarah Duffen Centre
Belmont Street
Southsea
Portsmouth
Hampshire PO5 1NA
Tel: 01705 824261 Fax: 01705 824265
E-mail: enquiries@downsnet.org
Website: www.downsnet.org/
Promotes the development of children and young people with Down's, and publishes information on training, a catalogue of books and educational materials.

Other useful addresses

ADD Information Services
PO Box 340
Edgware
Middlesex HA8 9HL
Tel: 0181 905 2013 Fax: 0181 386 6466
A charitable body which has links with over 150 ADD (Attention Deficit Disorder) support groups in the UK, and a mail-order service which supplies books and videos on ADD.

Advisory Centre for Education
Unit 1B Aberdeen Studios
22–24 Highbury Grove
London N5 2DQ
Tel: 0171 354 8321 (Mon–Fri, 2–5pm) Fax: 0171 354 9069
Offers free advice on issues related to education and special education.

AFASIC (Association for all Speech Impaired Children)
347 Central Markets
Smithfield
London EC1A 9NH
Tel: 0171 236 3632 (helpline) Tel: 0171 236 6487 (admin) Fax: 0171 236 8115
E-mail: info@afasic.org.uk
Website: www.afasic.org.uk
AFASIC is a source of information and support for chidren and young adults with speech and language impairments and their families. The association also organises conferences, activity weekends and parent groups, and has a publications and video list.

The Benefits Enquiry Line
Tel: 0800 882200
A free-phone number for parents seeking advice on financial benefits to which they may be entitled.

British Institute of Learning Difficulties
Wolverhampton Road
Kidderminster
Worcestershire DY10 3PP
Tel: 01562 850251 Fax: 01562 851970
E-mail: bild@bild.demon.co.uk
Publishes books and a journal, and provides training.

Carers National Association
20–25 Glasshouse Yard
London EC1A 4JS
Tel: 0171 490 8818 Fax: 0171 490 8824
As well as providing advice, the association has a network of support groups and produces publications on benefits and other practical matters.

Centre for Studies in Inclusive Education
1 Redland Close
Elm Lane
Redland
Bristol BS6 6UE
Tel: 0117 923 8450 Fax: 0117 923 8460
E-mail: 100432.3417@compuserve.com
Aims to increase the number of children with special needs in mainstream schools and produces a range of publications on inclusiveness.

Children's Legal Centre
University of Essex
Wivenhoe Park
Colchester
Essex CO4 3SQ
Tel: 01206 873820 (advice: Mon–Fri, 2–5pm) Tel: 01206 872466 (admin)
Fax: 01206 874026
E-mail: clc@essex.ac.uk
Runs a free legal advice and information service.

Child's Play (International)
Ashworth Road
Bridgemead
Swindon SN5 7YD
Tel: 01793 616286 Fax: 01793 512795
Suppliers of educational books, games, tapes and videos.

Contact a Family
170 Tottenham Court Road
London W1P 0HA
Tel: 0171 383 3555 Fax: 0171 383 0259
E-mail: info@cafamily.org.uk
Website: www.cafamily.org.uk
A charity which puts parents of children with medical or psychiatric problems in touch with parents of children with similar problems and with other useful organisations.

Department for Education and Employment (DfEE)
Elizabeth House
York Road
London SE1 7PH
Tel: 0171 510 0150

Hope Education
Orb Mill
Huddersfield Road
Waterhead
Oldham
Lancashire OL4 2ST
Tel: 0161 633 6611 Fax: 0161 633 3431
Suppliers of toys and equipment for children and those with special needs.

In Touch
10 Norman Road
Sale
Cheshire M33 3DF
Tel: 0161 905 2440 Fax: 0161 718 5787

IPSEA Independent Panel for Special Education Advice
22 Warren Hill Road
Woodbridge
Suffolk IP12 4DU
Tel: 01394 380518 (admin and fax) Tel: 01394 382814 (advice)
Offers legal advice for parents of children with special educational needs.

ISEA Independent Special Education Advice (Scotland)
164 High Street
Dalkeith
Mid Lothian EH22 1AY
Tel: 0131 665 7080 (advice)
The Scottish branch of IPSEA (see above).

Makaton Vocabulary Development Project
31 Firwood Drive
Camberley
Surrey GU15 3QD
Tel: 01276 681390 Fax: 01276 681368
This is the administrative centre for the Makaton signing system, which runs courses
on Makaton and produces a mail-order catalogue of publications and videos.

MENCAP
123 Golden Lane
London EC1Y 0RT
Tel: 0171 454 0454 Infoline: 0171 696 5593 Fax: 0171 608 3254
For all people with a learning disability and their families, MENCAP provides
support and advice at a local level and runs a leisure scheme for adults and children
with a learning disability.

National Association of Toy and Leisure Libraries: Play Matters
68 Churchway
London NW1 1LT
Tel: 0171 387 9592 Fax: 0171 383 2714
Website: www.charitynet.org/~NATLL
This is the head office for over 1000 toy libraries in the UK: send an SAE for details
of libraries in your area.

National Children's Bureau
8 Wakeley Street
London EC1V 7QE
Tel: 0171 843 6000 Fax: 0171 278 9512
Promotes the interests of all children through research, policy development and
encouraging good practice in education and social work. The bureau has a good
library and information service and publishes a book list and details of conferences.

NCH Action for Children
85 Highbury Park
London N5 1UD
Tel: 0171 226 2033 Fax: 0171 226 2537
Website: www.nchafc.org.uk
Projects include supporting children with special needs in the community, family centres, respite care and residential schools.

Nottingham Rehab
Ludlow Hill Road
West Bridgeford
Nottingham NG2 6HD
Tel: 0115 945 2345 Fax: 0115 945 2124
Suppliers, by mail-order catalogue, of household products, equipment, games and toys for those with special needs.

PLANET (Play Leisure Advice Network)
Cambridge House
Cambridge Grove
London W6 0LE
Tel: 0181 741 4054 Fax: 0181 741 4505
Website: www.oneworld.org/scf/planet
A source of information on play, leisure equipment, books, videos and suppliers, and will run a database search for your child's particular needs on request.

Pre-school Learning Alliance
69 King's Cross Road
London WC1X 9LL
Tel: 0171 833 0991 Fax: 0171 837 4942
E-mail: pla@pre-school.org.uk
Supports the establishment of community-run pre-schools, and provides information and training on special needs for helpers in these schools. Also gives grants to fund one-to-one helpers.

Riding for the Disabled Association
Lavinia Norfolk House
Avenue R
National Agricultural Centre
Stoneleigh Park
Kenilworth
Warwickshire CV8 2LY
Tel: 01203 696510 Fax: 01203 696532

ABOUT THE AUTHORS

Cheryl Rogers graduated from the University of Western Australia in 1979 with a Bachelor of Science degree, then trained as a journalist with Western Australian Newspapers Ltd. She worked for the weekly magazine *Countryman*, and spent two years overseas, which included working in England with the *Cambridge Weekly News* series. She lives with her husband Harry Gratte and their two children, Joel and Anna, in the Swan Valley, WA.

Gun Dolva met Cheryl during their studies at the University of Western Australia and graduated with a Bachelor of Science degree in Zoology in 1979. She went on to complete Honours and Masters degrees, and now works as sessional academic/tutor at Edith Cowan University. She is also involved in local environmental groups and has helped develop science enrichment activities for primary school pupils. She is Karina's mother and lives with her husband Rodney Potter and their three children, Danika, Karina and Joshua, in Darlington, WA.